LifeLight

"In Him was life, and the life was the light of men." John 1:4

2 Corinthians

LEADERS GUIDE

CONCORDIA PUBLISHING HOUSE • SAINT LOUIS

Pagan temples. Greek philosophy. A fractious, party spirit. These and other issues confronted Christ's Church in the city of Corinth. Continuing his apostolic care, and in anticipation of his impending visit, Paul sent them his second Spirit-inspired Pastoral Letter. Luther wrote, "In the first epistle, St. Paul rebuked the Corinthians severely for many things, pouring sharp wine into their wounds [Luke 10:34] and frightening them. But an apostle should be a preacher of comfort, to raise up terrified and fearful consciences, rather than to frighten them" (AE 35:383).

Depicted visually by people departing a pagan temple, leaving our former way of life is difficult. But Christ, through His cross and empty tomb, has set us free to be God's people. His Spirit "calls, gathers, and enlightens us" through the Gospel. Illustrated by the contemporary church building, we are God's new creation, because God has "reconciled us to Himself through Christ" (2 Corinthians 5:19).

3558 S. Jefferson Ave., St. Louis, MO 63118-3968
1-800-325-3040 • www.cph.org

Revised from material by Richard Kapfer, William Schmelder, and Frank Starr

Edited by Robert C. Baker

Denise Muhly, Laverne Schmidt, and Phyllis Sparks, field-test coordinators

Cover illustration by Steve Edwards © Concordia Publishing House

This publication may be available in braille, in large print, or on cassette tape for the visually impaired. Please allow 8 to 12 weeks for delivery. Write to Lutheran Blind Mission, 7550 Watson Rd., St. Louis, MO 63119-4409; call toll-free 1-888-215-2455; or visit the Web site: www.blindmission.org.

Manufactured in the USA

1 2 3 4 5 6 7 8 9 10   16 15 14 13 12 11 10 09 08 07

Contents

Introduction

Welcome to LifeLight

A special pleasure is in store for you. You will be instrumental in leading your brothers and sisters in Christ closer to Him who is our life and light (John 1:4). You will have the pleasure of seeing fellow Christians discover new insights and rediscover old ones as they open the Scriptures and dig deep into them, perhaps deeper than they have ever dug before. More than that, you will have the pleasure of sharing in this wonderful study.

LifeLight—An In-depth Study

LifeLight is a series of in-depth Bible studies. The goal of LifeLight is that through a regular program of in-depth personal and group study of Scripture, more and more Christian adults may grow in their personal faith in Jesus Christ, enjoy fellowship with the members of His body, and reach out in love to others in witness and service.

In-depth means that this Bible study includes the following four components: individual daily home study; discussion in a small group; a lecture presentation on the Scripture portion under study; and an enhancement of the week's material (through reading the enrichment magazine).

LifeLight Participants

LifeLight participants are adults who desire a deeper study of the Scriptures than is available in the typical Sunday morning adult Bible class. (Mid-to-older teens might also be LifeLight participants.) While LifeLight does not assume an existing knowledge of the Bible or special experience or skills in Bible study, it does assume a level of commitment that will bring participants to each of the nine weekly assemblies having read the assigned readings and attempted to answer the study questions. Daily reading and study will require from 15 to 30 minutes for the five days preceding the LifeLight assembly. The day following the assembly will be spent reviewing the previous week's study by going over the completed study leaflet and the enrichment magazine.

LifeLight Leadership

While the in-depth process used by LifeLight begins with individual study and cannot achieve its aims without this individual effort, it cannot be completed by individual study alone. Therefore, trained leaders are necessary. You fill one or perhaps more of the important roles described below.

The Director

This person oversees the LifeLight program in a local center (which may be a congregation or a center operated by several neighboring congregations). The director

- serves as the parish LifeLight overall coordinator and leader;
- coordinates the scheduling of the LifeLight program;
- orders materials;
- convenes LifeLight leadership-team meetings;
- develops publicity materials;
- recruits participants;
- maintains records and budgeting;
- assigns, with the leadership-team, participants to small discussion groups;
- makes arrangements for facilities;
- communicates outreach opportunities to small-group leaders and to congregational boards;
- follows up on participants who leave the program.

The Assistant Director *(optional)*

This person may assist the director. Duties listed for the director may be assigned to the assistant director as mutually agreeable.

The Lecture Leader

This person prepares and delivers the lecture at the weekly assembly. **(Lesson material for the lecture leader begins on p. 7.)** The lecture leader

- prepares and presents the Bible study lecture to the large group;
- prepares worship activities (devotional thought, hymn, prayer), using resources in the study leaflet and leaders guide and possibly other, outside sources;
- helps the small-group discussion leaders to grow in understanding the content of the lessons;
- encourages prayer at weekly leadership-team and discussion-leaders meetings.

The Small-Group Coordinator *(optional; the director may fill this role)*

This person supervises and coordinates the work of the small-group discussion leaders. The small-group coordinator

- recruits with the leadership-team the small-group discussion leaders;
- trains or arranges for training of the discussion leaders;
- assists the director and discussion leaders in follow-up and outreach;

- encourages the discussion leaders to contact absent group members;
- participates in the weekly leadership-team and discussion-leaders equipping meetings;
- provides ongoing training and support as needed.

The Small-Group Discussion Leaders

These people guide and facilitate discussion of LifeLight participants in the small groups. **(Lesson material for the small-group leaders begins on p. 57.)** There should be one discussion leader for every group of no more than twelve participants. The small-group discussion leaders are, perhaps, those individuals who are most important to the success of the program. They should, therefore, be chosen with special care and be equipped with skills needed to guide discussion and to foster a caring fellowship within the group. These discussion leaders

- prepare each week for the small-group discussion by using the study leaflet and small-group leaders guide section for that session **(see p. 57)**;
- read the enrichment magazine as a study supplement;
- guide and facilitate discussion in their small group;
- encourage and assist the discussion group in prayer;
- foster fellowship and mutual care within the discussion group;
- attend weekly discussion-leaders training meetings.

Leadership Training

LifeLight leaders will meet weekly to review the previous week's work and plan the coming week. At this session, leaders can address concerns and prepare for the coming session. LifeLight is a 1½-hour program with no possibility for it to be taught in the one hour typically available on Sunday mornings. Some congregations, however, may want to use the Sunday morning Bible study hour for LifeLight preparation and leadership training. In such a meeting, the lecture leader and/or small-group coordinator may lead the discussion leaders through the coming week's lesson, reserving 5 or 10 minutes for problem solving or other group concerns.

While it requires intense effort, LifeLight has proven to bring great benefit to LifeLight participants. The effort put into this program, both by leaders and by participants, will be rewarding and profitable.

The LifeLight Weekly Schedule

Here is how LifeLight will work week by week:

1. Before session 1, each participant will receive the study leaflet for session 1 and the enrichment magazine for the course. The study leaflet contains worship resources (for use both in individual daily study and at the opening of the following week's assembly) and readings and study questions for five days. Challenge questions will lead those participants who have the time and desire a greater challenge into even deeper levels of study.
2. After the five days of individual study at home, participants will gather for a weekly assembly of all LifeLight participants. The assembly will begin with a brief period of worship (5 minutes). Participants will then join their assigned small discussion groups (of twelve or fewer, who will remain the same throughout the course), where they will go over the week's study questions together (55 minutes). Assembling together once again, participants will listen to a lecture presentation on the readings they have studied in the previous week and discussed in their small groups (20 minutes). After the lecture presentation, the director or another leader will distribute the study leaflet for the following week. Closing announcements and other necessary business may take another five minutes before dismissal.

   In some places some small groups will not join the weekly assembly because of scheduling or other reasons. Such groups may meet at another time and place (perhaps in the home of one of the small group's members). Those congregations may record the lecture given by the lecture leader at the weekly assembly and duplicate it for use by other groups meeting later in the week.
3. On the day following the assembly, participants will review the preceding week's work by rereading the study leaflet they completed (and that they perhaps supplemented or corrected during the discussion in their small group) and by reading appropriate articles in the enrichment magazine.

Then the LifeLight weekly study process will begin again!

Recommended Study Resources

Concordia Self-Study Bible, New International Version. St. Louis: Concordia Publishing House, 1986. Interpretive notes on each page form a running commentary on the text. The book includes cross-references, a 35,000-word concordance, full-color maps, charts, and timelines.

Roehrs, Walter R., and Martin H. Franzmann. *Concordia Self-Study Commentary*. St. Louis: Concordia Publishing House, 1979. This one-volume commentary on the Bible contains 950 pages and is tailored for lay use.

Every Voice a Song Pipe Organ Accompaniment for 180 Hymns and Liturgy. St. Louis: Concordia Publishing House (order no. 99-1565). Use this music CD for worship hymn accompaniment.

God's Comfort in Affliction

2 Corinthians 1:1–11

Preparing for the Session

Central Focus

Paul found comfort in his afflictions from the God of all comfort, and Paul's own experience of this comfort overflowed into the comfort he passed along to the Christians of Corinth.

Objectives

That participants, led by the Holy Spirit, will

1. understand more fully the comfort we receive from God through the Gospel;
2. desire to share the comfort that overflows in our own lives as we are comforted by the God of all comfort; and
3. pass along to others in their sufferings the comfort with which we have been comforted by God.

Note for the small-group leaders: Lesson notes and other materials you will need begin on page 57.

For the Lecture Leader

Session Plan

Worship

Begin the session with the hymn printed in the study leaflet. Accompaniments are available in denominational hymnals, such as *Lutheran Service Book* or *Lutheran Worship* (refer to hymnal index). (Note: Concordia Publishing House has available *Every Voice a Song,* a 9-CD set of organ accompaniments for 180 hymns and liturgy. All the initial worship hymns in the LifeLight courses are included in this resource. It's especially helpful for mission congregations and small parishes. See the list of study resources on page 6.) Follow with the devotion.

Devotion

"I have said all these things to you to keep you from falling away. They will put you out of the synagogues. Indeed, the hour is coming when whoever kills you will think he is offering service to God. And they will do these things because they have not known the Father, nor Me. But I have said these things to you, that when their hour comes you may remember that I told them to you. I did not say these things to you from the beginning, because I was with you" (John 16:1–4).

St. Paul begins his second letter to the Corinthians by helping them to face up to the reality of affliction. Suffering for the faith did not come as a surprise to Paul. Jesus had warned His disciples before His own suffering on the cross that they would most assuredly face opposition and persecution for the faith. And He had warned that Paul personally would face these things (Acts 9:15–16). Apparently, this same kind of persecution had fallen on the Corinthian Christians.

Today, Christians in this nation do not ordinarily face physical danger for their faith. Yet it is clear that overt ridicule and criticism of Christian beliefs are not only increasing, but many of our neighbors accept it, approve of it, and even join in! And who among us has not suffered an illness, the death of a loved one, or a disappointment without also facing the nagging question of whether our faith could endure it?

This week's lesson focuses on afflictions—personal ones and societal ones. We will see what our Lord has to say to us about all this. And, then, with Paul, who had more than his share of suffering, we will be enabled to respond, "Through Christ our comfort overflows."

Prayer

Lord Jesus Christ, in the midst of the suffering or affliction that I must endure, help me to see Your loving hands in the comfort that others provide to me in Your name. Amen.

Lecture Presentation

Introduction

In the time of the apostles, when the Christian Gospel dawned upon the world with the brilliance of a clear sunrise and when the Church arose in the world with the freshness of a new day, all was peace and joy among believers. Right? Relationships between the apostles and those who became believers as a result of their message were always harmonious. Right? Wrong!

The picture of the Church in its earliest days that we find in Acts 2:42–47 and 4:32–35, where believers enjoyed a rich fellowship and shared unselfishly their worldly resources with one another and when the Church grew at a fantastic rate, is certainly inspiring and heartening. But even in the early chapters of Acts we find misunderstanding and discord entering into the life of the Church, even among the apostles themselves! (Recall the quarrel between Paul and Barnabas over Mark recorded in Acts 15:36–41.) In his letters, Paul finds it necessary to call upon Christians to forgive one another and to bear with one another patiently (e.g., Ephesians 4:31–32).

And then we have the church in Corinth! If you have taken part in the LifeLight course on 1 Corinthians, you are well acquainted with the internal problems troubling that congregation. Not only did the believers there have disputes with one another, but Paul's relationship with them was strained severely. In 1 Corinthians, Paul deals one by one with a long list of problems at Corinth. That letter was part of an ongoing process of working through these issues, a process which included not only Paul's letters but also a series of visits by Paul's representatives and by Paul himself. In this course, we will learn more about Paul's ministry to the Christians of Corinth, a ministry in which Paul appropriately, skillfully, and patiently applied Law and Gospel.

Because of the particular problems that troubled the Corinthian congregation and because of the challenge to Paul's apostolic authority, this letter is the most autobiographical to come from the apostle to the Gentiles.

> As an apostle Paul is a man in whom Christ speaks; he is the earthen vessel that conveys the treasure of the Christ. Paul is here fighting for his apostolate; that means, he is fighting for the Christ, for the apostolate is nothing less than the power and the presence of Christ among men. Men will find the treasure in this earthen vessel, or they will not find it at all; they will behold the light of the knowledge of the glory of God in the face of Christ in the apostolate, or they will not behold it at all. There is nothing like this letter to bind the church to the apostolic Word of the New Testament. The Reformation's embattled emphasis on *Sola Scriptura* finds powerful justification in this embattled epistle.
>
> Through conflict to triumph—Second Corinthians was born of conflict; and the triumph which Christ worked through it is not limited to the restoration of the Corinthian church of the first century. By it the church can triumph still.

2 Corinthians not only tells us a great deal about Paul, but it also helps us to understand the difficulties of a congregation bearing witness to the Gospel in a society that opposes it. Further, it shows how and why problems within a congregation must be dealt with in an evangelical and pastoral manner.

As we study this letter during the next nine weeks, we will consider it in three sections. In the first section (chapters 1–7), we will see how Paul deals with matters arising from his past relationship with the Christians of Corinth under the theme, "Paul's Authority and Ministry in Corinth." In the second section (chapters 8–9), we will see how Paul handles a present concern, the collection for the saints in Jerusalem. Then, in the third section (chapters 10–12), we will see how Paul prepares the Corinthians for an upcoming visit to them. As we begin now, let's review the setting in which this church found itself.

1 Circumstances Behind This Letter

A. The City of Corinth

Corinth was a major city on the Mediterranean Sea. It was located on a strip of land that connects the lower peninsula of Greece with southern Europe. This strip of land, the Isthmus, contributed its name to all other similar necks of land that separate two larger land masses; an isthmus is now any strip of land tying together two land masses and separating two seas. Its location provided Corinth with two ports, Cenchrea on the eastern sea and Lechaeum on the western sea. Since ships would have to sail a long way around the lower peninsula of Greece, goods would often instead be offloaded at one port, transported across the Isthmus to the other port, and loaded onto another vessel.

Its favorable location made Corinth a busy, prosperous city. It was a center of commerce, located at a crossroads, a place bustling with traders and travelers. At the time when Paul established the church there, the city of Corinth had a population of 250,000 free persons and 400,000 slaves. While there were many wealthy people in Corinth, the city also contained a substantial population of poor people—and it was from these that the church in Corinth was mostly—but not altogether—composed. (See 1 Corinthians 1:26.)

Corinth was a city of typical Greek culture. Established on a shelf 200 feet above sea level, it was bounded on the south by a towering rock (called the Acrocorinthus) 2,000 feet high. This rock had a summit extensive enough to permit a portion of the city to be built upon it. This area boasted structures even grander than those on the Acropolis of Athens. The city also boasted twelve temples, the most famous of which was the temple of Aphrodite, the goddess of love. This temple prided itself on its thousand prostitutes. So pervasive was the low moral climate that the Greek verb "to Corinthianize" meant "to practice sexual immorality."

B. The Church at Corinth

Paul founded the church at Corinth on his second missionary journey (AD 49–52). The story is told in Acts 18:1–18. Here Paul became acquainted with a Jewish Christian couple, Aquila and his wife Priscilla, with whom he stayed and with whom he worked. Later he was joined by Silas and Timothy. Paul spent eighteen months in Corinth, ministering to the people of God and becoming thoroughly acquainted with the membership and the problems of this important congregation.

During the third missionary journey, while Apollos ministered in Corinth, Paul spent his time in Asia Minor. While in Ephesus, Paul heard of problems in the Corinthian congregation, probably from the house of Chloe (about whom we have no other knowledge) and from others (1 Corinthians 1:11). In response, Paul wrote a letter that is now presumed to be lost (1 Corinthians 5:9). Sometime in AD 55, before the Jewish feast of Pentecost that took place in the spring, Paul wrote the letter from Ephesus that we know as 1 Corinthians. Timothy later returned from Corinth to Paul with a report about how the church had received this letter.

Paul then made a second visit to Corinth (2 Corinthians 13:1–2), which he later described as "painful" (2 Corinthians 2:1). Paul had promised to return to Corinth yet again when he finished his work in Ephesus. He originally intended to visit both before and after a visit to Macedonia. However, the difficulties in Corinth necessitated a change of plans. Paul did travel northward to Macedonia by way of Troas, but before leaving Asia he wrote a letter which apparently was severe in its tone (2 Corinthians 2:4). This letter could have been 1 Corinthians, but more likely it was another letter that has not been preserved.

Paul later received a report from Titus that contained both good and bad news. The good news was that the church had listened to Paul and obeyed him regarding the man who had fornicated with his father's wife (2 Corinthians 2:6; 7:7–16). The bad news was that not everyone had forgiven the offender (2 Corinthians 2:6), and that some still undermined Paul's authority (2 Corinthians 1:17, 23).

C. The Writing of 2 Corinthians

Paul wrote 2 Corinthians sometime during his third missionary journey (AD 52–56). During this time, the apostle spent three years ministering to the people in Ephesus—almost directly across the Aegean Sea from Corinth. In order to prepare the congregation for his third visit to Corinth, Paul penned this letter from Macedonia in AD 55, before the onset of winter. (If we presume that two of Paul's previous letters to Corinth have been lost, this letter would have been the fourth letter Paul wrote to this church.)

2 Salutation (1:1–2)

Paul greets the Corinthians in the typical letter-writing style of the day, but with his own personal touch. Since his apostolic authority has been questioned, Paul begins with a full-throated defense: he is an apostle of Christ Jesus through the will of God. His authority rests on the One whose he is and the One by whose will he carries out his apostolic office. He had used this kind of address before: "Paul, called by the will of God to be an apostle of Christ Jesus" (1 Corinthians 1:1). Paul was not another common philosopher roaming from one city to another and taking whatever profit he might and leaving his pupils behind. He was also not to be confused with the traveling opportunists who wandered in and out of Corinth. In this letter, Paul repeatedly will claim that his apostolic authority comes to him by the will of God, that he did not work among the Corinthians for his own profit, and that he did not come in his own power but in the power of the Gospel of Christ Jesus.

In spite of the many difficulties experienced by these people, which Paul will neither avoid nor condone, he still addresses the Corinthians congregation as "the church of God." They are "saints" who have been made holy and are continually kept holy in Christ Jesus together with all who call on the name of the Lord Jesus Christ. They are Christ's holy people—people, to be sure, who have a great deal of the old sinful nature still at work in their midst, but the people of God nonetheless. Because they are God's people, Paul the pastor will fully and freely apply both Law and Gospel to their situation.

So Paul greets them. His salutation involves a blessing that begins with the word *grace*. "Grace" means the divine favor of God, favor that is ours for the sake of Jesus Christ. To this *grace* he adds the word *peace,* the Hebrew greeting that includes a wish for health and wholeness. This kind of peace comes to us through our relationship to God by virtue of the covenant of His grace. This, in turn, brings healthy relationships between people. Grace and peace come from God our Father, who is our Father not only by creation, but also by salvation—He is our Father because He is the Father of our Lord Jesus Christ. In the incarnation, life, death, resurrection, and ascension of our Lord Jesus Christ, God the Father has made His grace and peace known.

Certainly we can be grateful for the truths expressed in these first two verses of this letter. We recognize that our wrongdoings and failings would disqualify us from belonging among the people of God. But God has extended His grace to each of us also through Jesus Christ, and, because this grace is available to us, we have peace with God. Because of Jesus, we belong among the saints who are holy to God and who by faith have received the righteousness of Christ as a gracious gift. Already in the salutation we hear the Gospel, the same Gospel Paul extends to this troublesome congregation at Corinth!

3 Comfort in Affliction (1:3–11)

Paul begins the content of his letter by giving praise to the Lord for comforting him in his affliction. He calls God the "Father of mercies." The word translated here as "mercies" (or "compassion") describes the love of God in the face of misery; it is the word for God's pity for those caught in a desperate situation. Paul also uses another word to refer to the way God has helped him. God is the "God of all comfort." This word "comfort" or "consolation"—"paraclete" in the original Greek, is a name applied both to the Holy Spirit and to the Lord Jesus. The word in either its noun or verb form appears ten times in verses 3–7. This God comforts us in our affliction, our distress, our tribulation—any troublesome outward circumstances.

Paul speaks from experience. An unbroken chain of tribulations have fallen upon the apostle (v. 4). (Perhaps Paul has in mind the tribulations that he later details in 2 Corinthians 6:4–10 and 11:23–33.) The Lord has comforted Paul and continues to do so. As a result, Paul is able to comfort others who are also in tribulation. He shares with them the same comfort with which he himself is being comforted by God. Note the marvelous chain we find here: God comforts us in our affliction; and by being comforted in this way we are enabled to comfort one another.

Paul notes that the sufferings of Christ flow over into our lives. This does *not* mean that we somehow suffer for our own sins and in this way have a share in saving ourselves. Rather, we share in the sufferings Christ experienced from the ungodly in this world—those sufferings that come to us because we are connected to Him. These are sufferings we bear for Christ's sake. But just as we share in the sufferings Christ experienced, we also share in the abundant comfort that flows from Christ (v. 6). So Paul maintains that the Corinthians will benefit from his affliction, since the comfort he receives from Christ will flow over into the comfort Paul is able to share with them. If Paul is being comforted, it is also for the sake of their comfort and salvation.

This comes about as the Corinthians share in the same sufferings Paul experiences. Since they share in the sufferings, they also will share in the comfort. Paul uses the word *share* twice in verse 7. The Greek word is the word that we also may translate as "communion." It means that we are partners. We take part in something with someone. The concept of such closeness, such *communion,* will become important later as this letter develops.

Paul does not write about ordinary afflictions (v. 8). When he refers to what was experienced in Asia, he no doubt is alluding to the riot which broke out in Ephesus as a result of his preaching. A silversmith named

Demetrius concluded that Paul's teaching would undermine the profits he and others derived from making small silver shrines to the goddess Artemis (Acts 19:23–41). Paul uses extremely expressive language as he explains the impact of the riot and its aftermath. Paul and those with him were heavily burdened by it—seemingly beyond their ability to withstand the pressure. They were at their wit's end. They despaired of coming out alive. But God had a purpose even in this. This conflict forced them to rely not on themselves, but "on God who raises the dead" (v. 10). As God had delivered them in the past, Paul was confident that God would continue to grant such deliverance in the future. Therefore, he and those with him set their hope on God.

On this basis, Paul appeals to the Corinthians to join in helping him through their prayers (v. 11). By supporting Paul and his colleagues in this way, the Corinthians will be helping the apostle bring to others the gift of God's grace in Christ that they themselves received. In turn, those who receive God's grace will thank God for the Corinthians and others whose prayers strengthened Paul and made it possible for him to keep on proclaiming the Gospel.

What a wonderful partnership we enjoy in the Gospel! We share with Christ and with one another the sufferings of those who remain faithful to God in an ungodly world. This, in itself, is a privilege—to join Christ in His suffering. But the benefits of that partnership go further still. We share also in the comfort, the consolation, that flows through Christ to us and through us to others. This comfort and consolation is anchored in—and leads us to—the eternal comfort and consolation of God's grace and peace in our Savior.

Conclusion

Paul begins 2 Corinthians on this encouraging note. With Spirit-inspired words, he now begins to bind up the still-painful wounds of this trouble-filled congregation. He will beckon them onward and upward along the bruising, stone-strewn pathway to the gates of God's glory. Let's follow!

Concluding Activities

Speak a brief prayer, perhaps asking God to bless leaders and participants as they journey together through this LifeLight course. Then make any necessary announcements and distribute study leaflet 2.

The Ministry of Divine Triumph

2 Corinthians 1:12–2:17

Preparing for the Session

Central Focus

Despite anxieties and pain as we serve Christ, we nevertheless participate in the divine triumph of the Gospel.

Objectives

That participants, led by the Holy Spirit, will

1. know that participation in the Church's Gospel ministry will involve pain as well as joy;
2. become more patient and trustful as God works through the Gospel; and
3. thank God for the wonderful privilege of having a place in the triumphant procession of the Gospel.

Note for the small-group leaders: Lesson notes and other materials you will need begin on page 59.

For the Lecture Leader

Session Plan

Worship

Begin the session with the hymn printed in the study leaflet. Accompaniments are available in denominational hymnals, such as *Lutheran Service Book* or *Lutheran Worship* (refer to hymnal index). (Note: Concordia Publishing House has available *Every Voice a Song*, a 9-CD set of organ accompaniments for 180 hymns and liturgy. All the initial worship hymns in the LifeLight courses are included in this resource. It's especially helpful for mission congregations and small parishes. See the list of study resources on page 6.) Follow with the devotion.

Devotion

"Now if anyone has caused pain, he has caused it not to me, but in some measure—not to put it too severely—to all of you. For such a one, this punishment by the majority is enough, so you should rather turn to forgive and comfort him, or he may be overwhelmed by excessive sorrow. So I beg you to reaffirm your love for him" (2 Corinthians 2:5–8).

In this week's lesson you noted the circumstance of a crushed and broken man. It is possible that he is the same person described in 1 Corinthians, the man who had had sexual relations with his father's wife (1 Corinthians 5:1–3). Assuming that this is the same person, the Corinthian Christians had heeded Paul's strong words and had condemned the man and his actions. They had accused and chided him so severely that he now stood on the brink of despair. Apparently no one had thought to speak to him the words of forgiveness and of new life in Christ.

Thus, Paul showed his pastoral heart by asking the Corinthians to forgive, restore, and love him. In this, Paul was reflecting the loving heart of our Savior.

Yes, God hates sin and calls sinners to repentance. But God doesn't leave us there! In fact, the sharp "No!" of God's Law is always preparatory to what God wants to say even more clearly and emphatically—the clear Word Paul calls "God's Yes." That "Yes!" is as clear as a man hanging on a cross. It is as certain as Easter's empty tomb. It is God's "Yes!" spoken to every sinner: "Yes, I love you! Yes, you are My child and heir. Yes, the Holy Spirit lives in you. Yes, you are accepted and enabled. Yes!"

This is why Paul, in the name of Christ, could say, "Forgive and comfort him." And by God's grace, those words of "yes" are spoken to us and through us to other sinners. So, with Paul, we say, "Amen," for the glory of God.

Prayer

Heavenly Father, thank You that through Jesus Christ You speak Your word of "Yes" to us, and help us to extend that word of grace, forgiveness, and acceptance to others. Amen.

Lecture Presentation

Introduction

Ministry can be painful. Christ's own ministry had been painful to Him. We think at once of the physical pain He suffered. He submitted Himself to an excruciating death—a slow, tortured death on the cross. But Christ also suffered anguish of soul. He cried out in that anguish as He suffered the wrenching separation from His Father. Remember His words? "My God, My God, why have You forsaken Me?" (Matthew 27:46). The heavenly Father withdrew from His Son, the Sin-Bearer.

Christ's suffering did not begin on the cross. He felt the pain of disappointment when some would no longer follow Him because they had no stomach for His teaching, the truths that He patiently explained and that had finally dawned upon them clearly. We can hear the disappointment in His voice as He turned to His disciples and asked, "Do you want to go away as well?" (John 6:67). We hear the sadness in Jesus' voice when He wept over His people's rejection of Him, "O Jerusalem, Jerusalem, the city that kills the prophets and stones those who are sent to it! How often would I have gathered your children together as a hen gathers her brood under her wings, and you would not! See, your house is left to you desolate" (Matthew 23:37–38).

Yes, the Savior knew pain of the heart as well as pain of the body. And so did His disciples and apostles. Paul knew bodily pain; he refers to it in 2 Corinthians 1:8–9 and talks about it at greater length in 6:3–10 and in 11:23–33. But Paul also knew heartache caused by those he loved. Much of our study this week has dealt with that heartache.

But, even in the pain of the body or heart, Paul exulted. He knew triumph. He rejoiced that God brings victory out of suffering, just as He had brought victory out of the suffering of Christ Himself. Paul concludes the section we studied this week by thanking God for giving him a part in the Lord's ministry of triumph. Let's look at that more closely for the next few minutes.

1 Paul's Conduct toward the Corinthians (1:12–14)

How frustrating it is to be misunderstood! How irritating it is to be misinterpreted! Yet Paul had to endure the malice of people who misinterpreted his letters and who read things into his life. Every one of these people ought to have been able to see otherwise. In response to such spiteful behavior, Paul appealed to his conscience. Paul's boast, the testimony of his conscience, was that he had conducted himself in the world—in his public activities and especially toward the Corinthians in his private dealings with them—in a manner that could stand up to God's own scrutiny.

One phrase of verse 12 in the English Standard Version reads "with simplicity and godly sincerity that are from God." Paul means that he has served the Corinthian believers without hypocrisy, without ulterior motives. In the clear light of day, his actions will pass God's inspection, not because Paul had tried so hard to develop these godly attitudes in himself, but because the grace of God had been at work in him. The foundation for his "boast" is not fleshly ("worldly") wisdom, but rather, the grace of God.

In reference to his conduct, Paul not only appeals to the integrity of his conscience, but he also appeals to the Corinthians' firsthand knowledge of that conduct among them. Paul writes only what the Corinthians can observe in his life, which they can take at face value. They can test his words by their own personal experience with him. In verse 13, Paul inserts a play on words. We cannot easily translate this into English, but in Greek the words translated "read" and "understand" are very similar. Paul is writing about something the Corinthians can both read and understand; there is no need to try to read between the lines.

If some in Corinth were getting only part of the message about Paul, it was because false apostles among them had distorted his clear statements. Paul hopes that his readers will understand him fully and thoroughly. Then (v. 14), when the Lord comes again, the Corinthians will be able to point to Paul's work among them because he brought them the Gospel of the forgiveness of sins. At that time, too, Paul himself will be able to point to the Corinthians as evidence that he has fulfilled the commission God gave him, and, in view of that evidence, the Lord will say to Paul "well done."

What a joy to any pastor to be able to say what Paul has said in defending his ministry to the Corinthians! To be able to appeal to a clear conscience concerning work that has been marked with holiness and sincerity, work that can stand up to God's inspection! To be able to point to the faith and growth in grace of a faithful flock! What a blessing!

2 The "Sore Spot"—Paul's Change in Travel Plans (1:15–22)

Paul knows that he has dealt faithfully and truly with the Corinthians—and thinks they know it, too, if they would but be honest with themselves. However, he faces the charge that he has been less than trustworthy. He now deals with that charge, that sore spot.

Some in Corinth had charged that Paul could not be trusted, that his word was not to be taken at face value. Here was the bone of contention: Originally, Paul had planned a single visit to the congregation (1 Corinthians 16:5). But then he had altered his plans to include a double visit, by which the Corinthians might benefit twice (v. 15). He had reached this decision as the result of careful deliberation, after weighing all of the possibilities. He planned to cross the Aegean Sea from Ephesus, landing directly at Corinth. After a brief stay in Corinth, he would go to Macedonia, and then return to Corinth so that the believers in Corinth could send him on his way to Judea with funds and supplies. Apparently, Paul had announced this double visit to the congregation, perhaps in a letter that we no longer have today, or perhaps by personal messenger.

Now, however, Paul had decided to revert to his original plan. Apparently, a serious situation in Macedonia demanded his immediate attention. There was "fighting without and fear within" (7:5). So his plans had been revised; he would first go to Macedonia and then to Corinth. Perhaps also Paul wanted to give the Corinthians time to work through their problems on their own so they might grow from the experience.

Whatever Paul's reasons for the changes, the troublemakers at Corinth used the apostle's change in plans as an opportunity to discredit Paul. They charged that he made his plans like a worldly man, prone to straddle the fence, trying to say yes and no at the same time (v. 17). But Paul was not double-tongued or irresponsible as they accused him of being—no more than the Gospel of Christ Paul had preached was untrustworthy. God does not vacillate when it comes to keeping His promises (v. 19). All the promises of God find their "yes," their fulfillment and affirmation, in Christ. This is why the Church responds with an amen and gives glory to God.

Turning his detractor's slander into an opportunity to accent the Gospel, Paul reminds the Corinthians that God gives a sure and certain salvation to all who are in Christ (vv. 21–22). Because of Christ (literally, the Anointed One), God has anointed us, marked us as His own, and placed His own seal upon us.

The picture Paul paints here is one of Holy Baptism. In Baptism, God anointed us with the Holy Spirit, just as He anointed Jesus in His Baptism. Furthermore, in Baptism, God has claimed us as His very own people. The Holy Spirit has come to live in us. His presence in our hearts is God's "guarantee," His "deposit," His "down payment," His "pledge" that He will finish the work He has begun in us. The word refers to earnest money to indicate sincerity in following through on a contract. The Holy Spirit is God's earnest money, the guarantee of His determination to carry through on the promises given to us.

What certainty and security God gives us in the Gospel of Christ!

3 The Reason for the Change (1:23–2:4)

After exposing the false charge that he was indecisive, Paul explains why he had changed his mind. He invokes God as his witness that he delayed his visit to them for the Corinthians' good, to spare them. In giving this explanation, Paul displays a genuine pastoral concern. He is not "lording it over" the Corinthians. He does not wish to dominate them by the sheer weight of his authority. Paul desires to work with them for their joy because they stand before God on the basis of their faith. Paul wishes to encourage and strengthen that faith. Paul the pastor seeks to train his congregation to use God's grace to stand on their own feet.

Paul could have used his apostolic authority and ordered the Corinthians to fall into line or else. This might have brought quicker results, but it might also have retarded their spiritual growth. Paul wanted the members of his congregation to grow in the grace and the knowledge of the Lord Jesus Christ, to become mature in their faith, to be responsible men and women in Christ.

Paul struggled with the decision to let them work out their own problem (v. 4). He wrote this letter "out of much affliction and anguish of heart and with many tears." He did not want to cause them pain. Rather, he wanted them to know his great love for them. Paul the pastor is here at work, with a compassion and love for the people entrusted to his care—a compassion and love he has himself experienced from Christ Jesus.

Pastors and other Christian leaders and counselors learn

the value of the same path taken by Paul. Oftentimes it seems easier to step in and make decisions *for* others. It looks more efficient and effective. But little or nothing will be learned by the one who is being "helped." Wise counselors provide guidance; they teach the kind of skills that will please God. But they let those they help make their own decisions and accept responsibility for those decisions. In this way, the one who is being helped also will be better prepared to make future decisions.

4 Dealing with the Repentant Sinner (2:5–11)

Paul now takes up a situation that has disturbed the congregation and where the congregation needs additional encouragement to bring it to a good conclusion. While he does not identify the situation precisely, we have every reason to link this section with the case of incest that Paul dealt with in 1 Corinthians 5:1–5. In that earlier letter, Paul expressed his dismay that the congregation had done nothing to discipline the offender. He directed the Corinthians to expel him from the church—just as Paul himself had already done as if he were among them. Paul explains in 2 Corinthians 2:5 that the whole congregation, not just Paul himself, had been hurt by the offense. Here we have the reminder that when one believer suffers, all suffer; when one part of the body suffers, the whole body experiences it.

But now this man has been brought to repentance, and it is not enough that the *majority* should extend forgiveness to him (v. 6). Rather, *all* must do this (v. 7). This must happen so that the repentant sinner does not become overwhelmed by excessive sorrow, so much sorrow that he is swallowed up and devoured by it. Forgiveness by all does not belittle the man's sin; instead, it underlines the grace of God that is ours in Christ. When a sinner has been brought to his knees, we are not to give the sinner an extra kick. No! When one is struck by the terrors of conscience brought about by the Law, then we must proclaim the grace of God in Christ Jesus without any conditions.

Paul himself sets the example in dealing with the sinner, just as he had done before. When the sinner had been unrepentant, Paul had pronounced his judgment on him (1 Corinthians 5:1–5). This man was to be delivered to Satan for the destruction of the flesh, so that his spirit might be saved in the day of the Lord Jesus. Now, however (v. 8), the congregation must solemnly confirm its love to the repentant brother.

The congregation is being put to a test. The question is not if they would obey Paul, but if they would act on the basis of the Gospel of Jesus Christ. The man who, while unrepentant, had been given over to Satan is now to be snatched back and preserved from the devil. Our Lord does not want His children to become the victims of Satan; we are not (v. 11) to be outwitted or defrauded by him. Satan is to be taken seriously, because we are not ignorant of his designs, his plots against the people of God—including his schemes to cause sinners to despair of God's grace!

We all need to learn this lesson well. We must not only be ready to condemn and expose sin so that those who are committing it see it for what it is, in all of its horror. But when sinners repent of their sin, we must also be ready and eager to restore them as dear brothers and sisters re-won for Christ and preserved for His kingdom. After all, Christ's kingdom is entirely filled with reclaimed sinners—beginning with us!

5 God Provides the Triumph (2:12–17)

Paul had found relief from the extreme anxiety he had experienced about the church in Corinth. Beginning in 2:12, he tells us about how that happened. Apparently he had sent Titus to Corinth to see how the congregation was doing in all their struggles. He had arranged to meet Titus in Troas, where he would receive a full report. But when Paul arrived there, he did not find Titus. That made Paul uneasy! Corinth, after all, was a key city for the advance of the Gospel.

Thus, even though Paul found an open door for the Gospel in Troas, it would have to wait. He had to make the Corinthians aware of his deep concern for them, so he went to Macedonia. What happened there Paul recounts beginning in 7:5.

But even before telling us about the relief he received in Macedonia about the Corinthians, Paul breaks into fervent thanksgiving to the Lord for giving him a part in the triumphant advance of the Gospel. God, Paul says, always leads us in triumph in Christ (vv. 14–16). In these verses, Paul calls up an image from his own times. The "triumph" was the celebratory procession granted by a Roman Caesar to a victorious general. The smell of flowers and garlands and incense would fill the air. To the vanquished prisoners marched along in disgrace or carried along the route in cages, all these scents were the smell of death. But to the victors it was indeed a sweet aroma. In the same way, the Gospel is Christ's triumph.

To those who are being saved, this Gospel is the fragrance of life leading to life!

Proclaiming the Gospel is a marvelous privilege—and an overwhelming task. Who is equal to it? We receive it only by God's grace. Yet, Paul notes (v. 17), some brashly take up the cause of the Gospel as if it were merchandise. They try to sell it at a profit. Paul and his coworkers were not "peddlers" of God's Word. The term refers to a huckster, even a shyster, one who deals in cheap merchandise, one who has the intention of making an unworthy profit, who handles his business deceitfully. Paul and his colleagues were not "peddlers." No, they were men whose actions would withstand the light of day, men sent by God, who with God's ever-present help speak the Word of Christ, in Christ's name.

Here is counsel for the Church today, and especially for those who hold the office of the public ministry. The Church must be above reproach. Our dealings must stand up under scrutiny. We are not hucksters of the Word of God; we are people who speak the very Word of Christ. Here on earth we will never reach perfection. Our motives and actions will never be completely pure this side of heaven. The evil one will continue to tempt and harass us. We will live together as God's people, warts and all.

But by God's grace, we listen to the Law of God, we repent of our sins, and we appropriate the full forgiveness and blessing of the Gospel for those sins. Then, and only then, are we fit to be those who speak to the world in the name of Christ.

Conclusion

Problems? Anxieties? Even pain? Yes, we still experience such things today, just as Paul himself did. Ministry has not become easier. But neither has it lost its share in God's triumph. We also take our place in God's victory parade, as the Gospel makes its way through the world into the hearts of those who will be saved. What a marvelous privilege is ours, also—a privilege that is worth the pain!

Concluding Activities

Speak a brief prayer, perhaps for the pastors and other church workers who serve the churches of the LifeLight participants. Then make any necessary announcements and distribute study leaflet 3.

Great Treasure in Earthen Vessels

2 Corinthians 3:1–5:10

Preparing for the Session

Central Focus

Though we have the ministry of the new covenant, which far exceeds the glory of the old covenant, we bear this treasure in the clay jars of our earthly existence. Even so, by God's grace, the glory of Christ shines through us to others.

Objectives

That participants, led by the Holy Spirit, will develop

1. a keener awareness of the surpassing glory of the Gospel;
2. a greater appreciation for the treasure of the Gospel even though it comes to us in the weak vessels of this earthly life; and
3. a greater sense of confidence and steadfastness in remaining faithful to the Gospel despite the hardships to which we are subject in this life.

Note for the small-group leaders: Lesson notes and other materials you will need begin on page 62.

For the Lecture Leader

Session Plan

Worship

Begin the session with the hymn printed in the study leaflet. Accompaniments are available in denominational hymnals, such as *Lutheran Service Book* or *Lutheran Worship* (refer to hymnal index). (Note: Concordia Publishing House has available *Every Voice a Song,* a 9-CD set of organ accompaniments for 180 hymns and liturgy. All the initial worship hymns in the LifeLight courses are included in this resource. It's especially helpful for mission congregations and small parishes. See the list of study resources on page 6.) Follow with the devotion.

Devotion

"But we have this treasure in jars of clay, to show that the surpassing power belongs to God and not to us" (2 Corinthians 4:7).

Before the age of banks and safe places to deposit money and precious possessions, people had to find safe hiding places in their homes or even in their fields. (Recall the parable Jesus told of the kingdom of God being like a treasure hidden in a field.)

The worst place in a home for hiding something precious would be an ornate box or jar. Such a container would immediately attract the attention of thieves. The best hiding place would be the most unlikely, perhaps a cracked or ugly jar.

Paul claimed to be just such a common clay jar. God had entrusted him with the treasure of the Gospel and had called him to share this treasure. Nevertheless, the Lord had chosen an ordinary, everyday container. The Lord had chosen Paul! God did this so that both Paul and his hearers would know that the power in the message of the Gospel came not from clay-jar Paul, but from the Lord Himself!

Time and again God uses clay pots for His mighty work: David, a shepherd boy through whom God slew Goliath; Joseph, a Hebrew slave who became second only to the Pharaoh; Moses, a stammering spokesman for the Lord; and Mary, a humble teenager whose body conceived and bore the Savior.

We sit on the same shelf as each of them—clay pots, all. And God chooses to use us just as He chose to use them, with all our cracks and smudges and weaknesses. He declares: "You shall be My witnesses!" As clay pots, like Paul, we thank God for choosing to use us, and we ask for His grace that we not get in the way of His powerful Gospel as we serve Him!

Prayer

Gracious God, thank You for choosing me—the earthen vessel that I am—as a witness to Your glorious grace in Christ Jesus, our Lord. Amen.

Lecture Presentation

Introduction

Have you ever been fooled by a gift you received because of the container in which it came? Perhaps a very small gift was wrapped in a very large box. Or a very large gift was presented to you in a very small container (as when a key to a new car is wrapped in a small box). Or a very expensive gift was wrapped very plainly. Sometimes the enjoyment of giving or receiving a gift is increased in this way by the added surprise.

In the Scripture section we studied this week, Paul refers to a very precious treasure contained in a very humble container. The treasure is new life in Jesus Christ; the humble container (which Paul calls a clay jar) is Paul himself—and the human ministers who bring the precious Gospel to people. What a contrast!

Actually, the verses we read were filled with contrasts. First, there is the contrast between the false teachers who present themselves by flashing impressive (though fake) letters of introduction and Paul, the genuine apostle, who offers no credentials except the results of his work in the hearts and lives of the Corinthians themselves. Then there is the contrast between the glory of the old covenant and the glory of the new covenant. Then the contrast between the treasure of the Gospel and the "clay jar" in which it comes. And finally there is the contrast between the tent of this earthly existence and the "permanent building"—the existence that will be ours in heaven. Throughout this section we are led to exclaim again and again, "What a contrast!"

1 Ministers of the New Covenant (3:1–18)

As we see from the Book of Acts, Paul, his associates, and the other apostles regularly and frequently traveled among the churches throughout the area we know as Asia Minor. Several of the New Testament epistles commend hospitality as a virtue. However, the apostles also warned churches to stand guard against false teachers and to refuse to receive them. Such false teachers were sometimes Jewish—non-Christian Jews intent on returning Christianized Jews to a Judaism that rejected Jesus, or Judaizing Christians intent on coercing evangelized Gentiles to be circumcised and to practice the Old Testament ceremonial law. (Paul and the other apostles regularly denounced such demands as undermining the Gospel.) Still other false teachers roamed the countryside attempting to make a profit from the Gospel by charging for their teaching or abusing the generosity of Christ's people.

Because traveling apostles, evangelists, prophets, and teachers might be personally unknown to the congregations they visited, they sometimes presented letters of introduction to win acceptance. False teachers were not above forging such documents. This had apparently happened in Corinth, where false teachers presented letters of recommendation for themselves while attempting to discredit Paul since he carried no letters of introduction.

But Paul and his coworkers, ministers of the new covenant of the Gospel, did not need to commend themselves again to the Corinthians. They did not need letters of introduction. Paul had already worked among the Corinthians; in fact, he had established the congregation (Acts 18:1–8). Why, the Corinthians themselves were the only "letters" Paul needed to commend the authenticity of his apostleship (v. 2)! Their very faith showed that they were a "letter" from Christ delivered by Paul and his coworkers. These letters were not written with ink, but by the Spirit of the living God (v. 3). The message they bore was not written on paper—not even on tablets of stone (the medium of the Ten Commandments, the foundation of the old covenant delivered to Israel through Moses). Rather, God had written His message on the hearts of the Corinthians themselves.

Nevertheless, even though Paul had accomplished much in Corinth, he does not claim to be qualified as a minister of the Gospel on the basis of his own competence. He is qualified only (v. 5) because God has qualified him to be a minister of a new covenant. Paul's confidence rests in what God had done and continued to do through him.

From these opening verses of chapter 3, Paul now turns to a discussion of the glory of the new covenant of which God has made him a minister. But, as we continue with this topic, it is important that we understand the meaning of the word *covenant*, both in the Old and the New Testaments. The covenants God has made with people are different from the covenants we are used to. In everyday speech, we frequently use the word *covenant* to refer to a contract, a bilateral agreement, something to which two sides pledge adherence.

When God makes a covenant with people, this is not the case. God makes unilateral covenants, one-way covenants. He is the active party, the initiator; His people are passive participants, the recipients of the blessings that God freely bestows through His covenants.

God had made a conditional covenant with Israel at Mount Sinai. This covenant promised life and blessing to those who would keep it. There was nothing wrong with this covenant. Nevertheless, it resulted in death because neither the Israelites nor anyone else could keep it. Our sinful nature—the sinful nature all human beings have inherited from Adam—made our obedience to God impossible. Nevertheless, because it was God's covenant, the covenant made at Sinai had a splendor, a brightness that caused the face of Moses to glow. Moses physically reflected the glory of God that shone from the "old covenant," the covenant made at Mount Sinai (v. 7). The people of Israel could not look upon the face of Moses when he came from the presence of God, where he received the Ten Commandments, so Moses put a veil over his face.

Paul reminds his readers of that veil. He explains that it represents a veil that to this day continues to keep many people from seeing the glorious truth that God's old covenant revealed—our need for a Savior from sin, a Savior whom God promised to send (vv. 12–14). That veil is the sin of unbelief. When someone comes to faith in Christ, the veil is removed.

Now, if the old covenant—a covenant which brought condemnation and death because no one could keep it—had splendor, how much more splendor belongs to the new covenant God has made with us through Jesus (vv. 10–11)! For, instead of bringing death, this new covenant brings righteousness—a right standing with God based on the holy life and death of Christ Himself. And, unlike the old Mosaic covenant, the splendor of which faded away, the splendor of the new covenant is permanent, eternal.

The Law remains God's good and gracious will; nevertheless, the Law, when it comes into contact with our sinful nature, always accuses. But what the Law could not do, God has done in Jesus Christ. His righteousness has been made known in the death and resurrection of His Son. And this supersedes any word of Law, because God has spoken His final and ultimate word in the Word who was made flesh.

Because this is the nature of the new covenant that God has made with us in Christ, the testament in His blood, we are very bold. We don't need a veil over our faces. Rather, unveiled—open faced—we reflect the glory of God (v. 18). We reflect the Gospel as a mirror reflects objects before it. And this reflection is becoming more and more clear as we are being changed more and more into the likeness of Jesus. We are being transformed into Christ's image more and more as the Holy Spirit works in our hearts and our lives by the Gospel; we reflect more and more accurately the glory that God has shown to us in the face of Jesus Christ. This transformation is not our doing; we can take no credit for it. The changes come to us from the Lord who is the Spirit, the Spirit who continues to enlighten the people of God and keep us united in Christ in the one true faith.

2 Earthen Vessels (4:1–15)

The splendor of the new covenant is the Gospel of God's grace. It far outshines the glory of the old covenant. This grace of God in the Gospel is the source of great confidence for the people of God. Since God has shown us mercy, compassion, and pity in Christ, we do not wear ourselves out in our struggle with sin and with the troubles of this life. We do not lose heart. God's power and grace are ours in the Gospel. So we have renounced every strategy, every form of presenting the Gospel that is underhanded or deceptive (v. 2). We refuse to resort to trickery. We don't tamper with the Word of God. We will not adulterate it. We will not disgrace the Gospel of Jesus Christ by attempting to sell it as entertainment. Rather, by openly proclaiming the truth, by openly presenting the Gospel in all its unveiled brightness, we would commend ourselves in the sight of God.

If our Gospel seems to be veiled, it is only veiled to those who are perishing (v. 3). This is because the god of this world (Satan) has blinded the minds of the unbelievers to keep them from seeing the light of the Gospel of the glory of Christ, who is the likeness of God. Proclaiming the Gospel of Jesus Christ is the business of the Church; creating faith in that Gospel is not. The Holy Spirit creates faith where and when it pleases God.

Paul says that we preach, not ourselves, but Jesus Christ as Lord (v. 5). The same God who in the beginning spoke and caused light to spring out of darkness has now shone His Gospel into our hearts to give us the light of the knowledge of His glory in the face of Jesus Christ. There is the magnificence of God's enlightening the world. His glory has been revealed to us in the light of the knowledge of what He has accomplished for us in the person and work of His Son. He is indeed the true light who enlightens everyone coming into the world; He is the light of the world.

We have this treasure in clay pots, in breakable jars, in earthen vessels. The great treasure of the Gospel comes to us in ordinary, mundane containers. The Lord continues to relate to His Church through ordinary means, the ordinariness of other human beings—the most ordinary and everyday kinds of utensils. But this, in itself, communicates something about the Gospel. The clay jars underscore the truth that the treasure comes from God and never from us.

Paul now further illustrates this truth by introducing four pairs of contrasts (vv. 8–9). First, he says, we are afflicted in every way but are not squeezed into a corner. Second, we are at a loss but not in despair. Third, we are persecuted but not forsaken. Fourth, we are knocked down but not knocked out. None of the afflictions Paul endured could ever stop him from preaching the Gospel. No wonder that later in this book Paul will exclaim that when he is weak then he is strong (12:10). Jesus lives in us, His Church, and He is working through us. Jesus' suffering and death are reflected in the suffering and death Christians endure as His servants and for His sake.

But Jesus' life, His victory through suffering and death, and His triumph over suffering and death also are reflected in His Church. This is what Paul means when he writes that we "are always carrying in the body the death of Jesus, so that the life of Jesus may also be manifested in our bodies" (v. 10). The many hardships Paul faced in his ministry may have revealed the mortality of his body, but this was so the life of Jesus might be even more evident. Death may have been at work in him, but this resulted in life for his hearers. This was Paul's task: to bring life to the Corinthians, even if it meant death for his body.

Even if the Corinthians did not always understand Paul, even if they charged him with being less than they thought an apostle should be, Paul did not grow weary serving as a minister of the Gospel of Jesus Christ. After all, Paul's hardships only served to show the extraordinary quality of power that belongs to God, and not to Paul.

3 Confidence (4:16–5:10)

Paul does not lose heart. Outwardly, he might be wasting away. He will detail the demands of his difficult ministry later (11:16–33), and these demands and hardships have taken their toll. But inwardly Paul is being renewed every day. So too with us. While we may not "bear in our bodies the marks of the Lord Jesus" in the same way Paul did, we know the frailties of our humanity, and we witness the wasting away of our own bodies and the bodies of loved ones. But we also know that each day in our Baptisms the new nature in Jesus Christ arises. That nature lives before God in righteousness and purity now and forever. It becomes new again day after day.

Whatever we must face in the way of affliction is only momentary and lightweight, and it works out for us in an eternal weight of glory that is of extraordinary quality (v. 17). This does not mean that we receive glory because of our afflictions; the glory we will receive comes only by the merits of Jesus. Yet, in the hand of God, affliction becomes the instrument for working out the glory. We are looking not for what may be seen, but for the unseen (v. 18). Our focus is not on what happens to us in this life but on the life to come. What we see lasts only for a time; what we do not yet see will last for eternity.

For we know (5:1)—and here Paul does not use the word which means "to know from experience," but "we know from God's revealing it"—that if our earthly tent-house, our restless, impermanent tenting, is destroyed, we have a building, a permanent dwelling not made by human hands but made for us in heaven by God.

"For here we do not have an enduring city, but we are looking for the city that is to come" (Hebrews 13:14). While we live here in this temporary shelter of our earthly existence, we long for the permanence of our heavenly dwelling. While we live here on earth, we groan (v. 2). Here and now, we find ourselves burdened, weighed down, but not with the weight of glory we read about earlier (4:17). We do not want to strip off the flimsy existence we have now, but rather we want to put on the permanent existence God has promised we will have. We want our mortality swallowed up by life. Here Paul echoes the words of 1 Corinthians: "Death is swallowed up in victory" (1 Corinthians 15:54).

Paul elsewhere expressed the desire to depart and to be with Christ, for that is far better (Philippians 1:23). And the One who has worked this out for us is God, who has given us the Spirit as a down payment of what He will give us in all its fullness in the life to come.

Therefore, we have unlimited confidence. We know that as long as we are at home in the body—as long as we are in this life—we are away from our home with the Lord—we are not yet in our heavenly home. Sometimes we read or hear the phrase, "absent from the body, present with the Lord," in an obituary or when a death is announced. This expression is a confession of our Christian faith. We are confident about God's promises of eternal life in heaven, and we look forward to that day when we will leave this life behind for life in our permanent, heavenly home.

But whether we are at home or away, we have one aim: to please God. We know that we must all appear before the judgment throne of Christ to receive punishment or reward according to what we have done in the body. This is hardly work righteousness. Rather, what we do in the body is the evidence that our faith in Christ has been genuine. Paul's words parallel those of Jesus regarding the last judgment (Matthew 25:1–46).

As Paul stood on trial before Felix, he declared his hope in the resurrection of the just and of the unjust. This hope, he said, led him continually to keep his conscience clear toward God and toward men (Acts 24:15–16). As much as any person presented in the Bible, Paul knew the impossibility of perfection; he testified that he himself was still pressing on toward the goal of Christlikeness (Philippians 3:12–14); he knew the wretched agony of being caught in the grip of his own sinful nature (Romans 7:24). All the more, then, Paul gave thanks to God through Jesus Christ because he had been delivered from this body of death (Romans 7:25). So he did not lose heart.

Conclusion

Contrasts? Yes, there are plenty of contrasts in the life of a Christian. Treasure in clay jars. The Gospel contrasts so markedly with the vessel that bears it. What we are contrasts sharply both with what we deserve and with what we hope to be. What we have now stands in stark contrast with what we hope to have in eternity. Yet these contrasts do not disprove our Christian hope. Instead, they prove the certainty of that hope. These very contrasts define the Gospel. Think of it: clay jars bear the treasure, and the treasure will one day transform the jars of clay.

Concluding Activities

Speak a brief prayer, perhaps thanking God for the hope we have through the Gospel. Then make any necessary announcements and distribute study leaflet 4.

The Ministry of Reconciliation

2 Corinthians 5:11–6:10

Preparing for the Session

Central Focus

A wonderful change has come about in our relationship with God since Christ has reconciled us to God. As the Lord's ambassadors and fellow workers with Christ, we implore others to be reconciled to God through faith in Christ.

Objectives

That participants, led by the Holy Spirit, will

1. know more deeply the fear and love of God that convinces us that Christ died for all and compels us to share the Gospel with others;
2. appreciate the privilege Christ has given us in making the Gospel known; and
3. show great endurance in commending the Gospel to others.

Note for the small-group leaders: Lesson notes and other materials you will need begin on page 64.

For the Lecture Leader

Session Plan

Worship

Begin the session with the hymn printed in the study leaflet. Accompaniments are available in denominational hymnals, such as *Lutheran Service Book* or *Lutheran Worship* (refer to hymnal index). (Note: Concordia Publishing House has available *Every Voice a Song,* a 9-CD set of organ accompaniments for 180 hymns and liturgy. All the initial worship hymns in the LifeLight courses are included in this resource. It's especially helpful for mission congregations and small parishes. See the list of study resources on page 6.) Follow with the devotion.

Devotion

"Working together with Him, then, we appeal to you not to receive the grace of God in vain. For He says, 'In a favorable time I listened to you, and in a day of salvation I have helped you.' Behold, now is the favorable time; behold, now is the day of salvation" (2 Corinthians 6:1–2).

If only . . . Those are two of the saddest words human beings can speak. They express regret, guilt, and sorrow:

If only I hadn't lost my temper . . .

If only I could take back my words . . .

If only I had spoken up when I had the chance . . .

Probably most of us have thought or voiced regrets like these. In the reading you did for today, you may have noticed the pleading tone in Paul's words to the Corinthians. He pleads with them because he wants to prevent their ever having to say, "If only . . ." as they mourn a decision to ignore God's call to repent and live.

It's so easy to think of our Christian faith as having to do only with life after death, with God's promise that we will live with Him forever in the heavenly home when our life here on earth ends. That promise truly does belong to us and we rejoice in it.

But consider the other benefits believers receive from God—benefits we receive from Him right here and now. Paul writes, "Therefore, if anyone is in Christ, he is a new creation. The old has passed away; behold, the new has come" (2 Corinthians 5:17). When we come to faith, we begin life anew! We carry that newness into our homes and marriages, into our jobs and friendships. Everything can look different to us, because in reality everything *is* different. We see our life no longer merely "according to the flesh" (2 Corinthians 5:16), but through brand new eyes.

How many times people have said with a tinge of regret, "I wish I had known Christ sooner. I've wasted so much time. I could have lived so much more freely and meaningfully. If only I had known!"

Paul himself had lived without the Gospel for a long time prior to his conversion. He knew what it meant to live as an enemy of God. He knew the relief of having the scales lifted from his eyes, the relief of being spiritually reborn to live as God's new creation in Christ.

That's why he wrote these urgent words: "We implore you on behalf of Christ, be reconciled to God" (2 Corinthians 5:20).

For us as for Paul, the old has gone. The new has come. Christ has nailed the "if only" events of our lives to His cross. He has made us God's new creation, for whom the "if only's" need be only a distant memory.

Prayer

Precious Savior, help me to drop the heavy load of the "if only's" of my life at the foot of Your life-bestowing cross. Amen.

Lecture Presentation

Introduction

Certainly one of the most beautiful services anyone can perform is to bring enemies together—to reconcile them. How heartwarming when former friends who have had a falling out are brought together again and their friendship is rekindled! What a great relief over a tragedy averted when an estranged couple can be brought together and renew their love and devotion! What a joy when a nation divided by clashing interests and loyalties comes together on rediscovered common ground and goals! Reconcilers provide a wonderful service for those they bring together.

And the greatest reconciler of all is Christ! For Christ has reconciled us to God by His sacrificial, atoning death. Notice that I did not say that Christ reconciled God to us. For it was not God who had moved away from our relationship with Him; rather, *we* moved away from God when we sinned—through our first parents Adam and Eve and through our own individual sin. Christ reconciled us to God—brought us back to God—through His atoning work. Reconciled to God in Christ, we are now enlisted in the great ministry of reconciliation. We have become ambassadors of Christ, commissioned to share the wonderful message of reconciliation.

1 The Love of Christ: Reason for Persuasion (5:11–13)

What is the heart of the Gospel? What teaching of the Christian faith is so crucial that the Church stands or falls by it? Certainly this: that we are justified, made right, before God by His gracious love and forgiveness for Christ's sake through our faith in His redeeming work. This truth is the foundation of our relationship with God. Theologians say this teaching is the basic principle of Christianity. It is the core message of the Sacred Scriptures. This is the message that we believe, teach, and confess before the world.

In the section of 2 Corinthians we studied this week, Paul shows how thoroughly his ministry in Corinth has been shaped by this central Gospel teaching—that Christ has reconciled us to God. Paul calls on the Corinthians to receive this gracious message of God with faith.

God had given Paul the task of winning people to faith in Christ. The apostle worked tirelessly to persuade people to believe that God is gracious to us for Christ's sake. Paul did what he did because (v. 11) he knew the fear of the Lord. As Paul uses the phrase here, "fear of the Lord" does not mean that Paul lived in terror of God. He did not do what he did because he was afraid of what God would do to him if he didn't do it. Paul did not cringe before his God as if avoiding the blows of a whip.

Rather, the word *fear*, as Paul uses it here, stresses a reverence for God that grows out of knowing what God has made known. Paul is referring especially to knowing the glory of God's grace that shines clearly in the Gospel message. As Paul explained in chapter 3, this glory—the glory of the new covenant—far surpasses the glory of the old covenant. That covenant, given at Sinai, did indeed have a glory all its own. The Law was holy, just, and good, as Paul wrote to the Christians in Rome. However, that conditional covenant demanded that human beings perfectly obey God's Law. As we saw in a previous session, no human being could do that. So God, in love, has given us a new covenant, the covenant of His grace based in the forgiveness of all sin because of what Jesus Christ did for us in His life, death, and resurrection.

When Paul talks about the fear of the Lord, he means the awe and reverence we experience when we realize all that our Lord has done for us. This fear is the beginning, or foundation, of wisdom. The Lord is gracious and compassionate, and He has redeemed His people (Psalm 111). Believing that, Paul cannot help but declare the Gospel.

Paul knew who he was before God—for he now knew himself in the light of the Gospel of God's grace. Paul wanted the Corinthians to see him in that light, too, just as God did (vv. 11–12). Paul hopes that they will have the honesty to acknowledge him as what they know him in their consciences to be—an authentic apostle of the Lord (v. 12). Paul does not intend to begin commending himself to the Corinthians all over again. Instead, he appeals to them to acknowledge what they already know about him and to stand with him against those who pride themselves on outward appearances and not on what is in the heart.

Perhaps Paul did not measure up to the standards set up by those false teachers for whom outward appearances were everything. Perhaps his costume was not of the fashionable cut of a professional man. Perhaps he did not groom himself so as to win the admiring glances of potential followers. Perhaps his diction and speaking style betrayed common origins. Perhaps his willingness to soil his hands with manual labor to support himself did not make the right impression.

But Paul did not ask to be judged by outward appearances. Paul asked to be judged by what came from his heart, by what motivated his behavior toward the Corinthians. False teachers might consider Paul's wholehearted giving of himself to his ministry insane (v. 13). Nevertheless, Paul had done it for Christ; he would not hold back in his service to God, even if doing so seemed like insanity to others who did not have faith or know what it means to live as the Lord's faithful steward.

What zeal Paul must have shown! And what a challenge to us as we evaluate our own lives. Perhaps we could learn from Paul's wholehearted service. Are we only too ready to let public opinion guide our actions? Are we too prone to watch the polls as we make decisions? Have we made such full use of God's grace to live for Christ that those around us consider our commitment fanatical or even insane? These are sobering questions, which prompt each of us to examine our relationship with our Lord, to take inventory, and to spend time in prayer, asking our Lord for pardon and for increased zeal.

2 The Love of Christ: One Died for All (5:14–15)

Such an exercise can drive us to despair unless we remember what motivated every aspect of Paul's ministry: the love of Christ (v. 14). The word translated "controls" (or "compels") means to hold in one's grip. What is this Christlike love like? We need only look at Christ Himself to find the answer. He died for all. Christ's love went to the cross. His own sins did not send Him there. Rather, He carried the sins of the world with Him to that cross. Christ did not die because *He* deserved it, but because *we* deserve it. Christ died on behalf of us all.

No wonder Paul felt Christ's love "controlling" him to do what he did. Love like that cannot help but change us. It surely changed Paul. Just think of it! Jesus Christ died in our place and for our benefit. That would surely be enough to motivate us to live in love toward others. But we still would lack the power to do so.

That's why Paul goes on to reveal another wonderful truth. When Jesus died, we died with Him! Scripture assures us (Romans 6:1–11) that in the waters of Holy Baptism our old sinful nature was drowned and died. This old sinful self is now dead and gone as far as God is concerned. Instead, when God looks at us He sees the new person we now truly are—a new person covered in the righteousness of Jesus (Galatians 3:26–27). We have a new life to live before God, a new life that is guided and directed by the Holy Spirit through the Gospel (Romans 8:9–11).

What good news this is! What an encouragement and powerful inducement to dedicate ourselves to live for God! People for whom Christ died are no longer to live for themselves but for Him who for their sake died and was raised. The love of Christ has its grip on us, and the love of Christ guides and directs our relationships with one another.

3 Reconciliation: A New Relationship with God (5:16–19)

So we no longer regard one another "according to the flesh." We no longer judge other people by their social, political, or financial standing; by physical considerations like age, health, or gender; by nationality or race; or by any of the other standards people in this world commonly use to evaluate one another. Paul confesses (v. 16) that he once even measured Christ using those kinds of standards. Before Paul's conversion on the Damascus road, he saw Jesus in quite a different light, a worldly light.

But no longer! Paul's evaluation of Christ did an abrupt about-face when he came to know Jesus as his Savior and Lord. This same experience also abruptly and decidedly changed the way Paul regarded everyone else. Every other person who comes to know Christ as Paul knew Him undergoes the same kind of change Paul did (v. 16). God changes us. We now worship and honor Christ as our Savior and Lord. And we now regard one another in love as those for whom Christ died. Fellow believers become brothers and sisters in the Lord. We now live (v. 17) "in Christ," as God's new creation; the old is gone, the new has come.

God has not changed His mind about His judgment on

sin. Nor have we stopped being sinners. What has changed is our status before God. God shifted our sin to Christ, and He shifted Christ's righteousness to us. God Himself brought about this change (vv. 18–19). Our change in status does not begin with our desire to have a new relationship with God, but with God establishing a new relationship with us through the Gospel in Word and Sacrament. Christ is the instrument God used to bring about reconciliation. The grace of God—His undeserved love and favor—is located in His Son. He is the only one in whom we find reconciliation. God has done the reconciling through Him, and through the means of grace brings that reconciliation personally to us.

Reconciliation. When we use this word, we usually mean that two parties to a dispute are brought together, each one contributing to the restoration of a relationship. We know about reconciliations that have taken place between husband and wife, labor and management, or nation and nation. In such cases, each side has to give a little. Unless both are willing to work at it, reconciliation is impossible.

However, such imagery from human relationships falls short when we think of the reconciliation Christ has brought about between us and God. This reconciliation is one-sided—God alone does it all. It's one way—God reconciles us to Himself. He does it through Christ. He does it for the world. In Christ, the whole world has been reconciled to God.

What wonderful news! Now our sin no longer stands between us and our God! Now we need not tremble in terror when we think about the coming judgment! For Christ's sake, the debt of sin we had incurred is gone. Not only has Christ paid the penalty for our sins, He has given us in exchange (v. 21) His own righteousness. Thank God!

4 Paul's Ministry of Reconciliation (5:20–6:10)

This is good news for us and for everyone! God has reconciled the whole world to Himself through Christ on His cross. Now that by His grace we know and believe this glorious news, we can't help but pass it along to others. The ministry of reconciliation (vv. 18–19) God gave to Paul amounts to nothing short of a divine appointment to service in God's kingdom. Christ's ambassadors (v. 20) speak the King's message: God no longer counts people's sins against them. That's the Gospel—the Good News that God forgives sins for the sake of Christ.

God called Paul to be an ambassador, Christ's personal representative to this world. What a commission! Think, now, about an ambassador's commission. An ambassador is sent to represent not his or her own views but the views of the government he or she represents. Ambassadors are charged with the privilege and the responsibility of delivering the messages of those who sent them.

Paul understood that charge. Paul was *Christ's* ambassador. Paul knew that, through him, Christ was addressing the world with His redeeming Gospel. And Christ continues to do this still today. He has commissioned His Church to deliver His message of forgiveness and reconciliation to all nations.

What an exciting calling God has given to us as His Church! We represent the Savior to a world that desperately needs Him; we have a wonderful message to share—an authoritative message backed by Christ Himself! Jesus has promised, "If you forgive the sins of anyone, they are forgiven; if you withhold forgiveness from anyone, it is withheld" (John 20:23). What a message of reconciliation! What a responsibility! What a thrilling task!

So Paul pleads with the Corinthians (v. 20) to be reconciled to God. He appeals on behalf of Christ, the holy Savior who knew no sin, but who, for our sake, became sin and who has now given us His right standing before the Father. Christ knew no sin. He alone is holy, harmless, undefiled, and separate from sinners (Hebrews 7:26). But (note the precise wording—v. 21) God made Him to *be* sin; the Lord laid on Him the sins of us all (Is. 53:6). As a result we, who know sin only too well, are made the righteousness of God in Christ. God has transferred our sins to Christ, who paid for them on the cross, and God has transferred Christ's righteousness to us. Because of Christ, God sees us as having His own righteousness.

As those whom God has called to be His helpers (6:1), Paul and his associates implore the Corinthians to exploit the wonderful opportunity they now have to receive God's grace. Paul pleads with them not to receive the grace of God in vain. That can happen. If we live self-centered lives (5:15), God's grace is wasted. If we attempt to earn God's favor on our own, we've received God's grace in vain. Either approach empties grace of its power and renders it meaningless.

Just as the Holy Spirit pleaded with the Corinthians, so also He addresses His urgent plea to us. We also enjoy the wonderful opportunity to receive God's grace. We, too, have received the Gospel message; none of us wants to give it up or let God's grace pass us by! Maybe we have not let God have His way in our hearts. Maybe we have merely assented in an intellectual way to the Gospel. Maybe we have never taken God's grace seriously. Maybe we have exhausted ourselves trying to make ourselves somehow worthy of His love. The opportunity to rejoice in God's grace has come to us now. Now is the right time. Now is the decisive moment.

We cannot safely postpone the attention our souls need. We dare not wait for some better time, some more convenient time. We may say to ourselves, "After I get more settled in this job, after I have accomplished my career and family goals, after the children are grown, after I retire . . ." We may try to put God's grace on the back burner of our hearts. And we may succeed. But we cannot safely postpone an encounter with Christ. *Now* is the right time. *Now* is the day of salvation.

Paul felt the pressure of that reality in his own work as Christ's ambassador. In the Greek, he uses a double negative (6:3) to emphasize his point. An English translation is, "We put not obstacles in anyone's way." Paul refuses to damage or hinder the faith of anyone for whom Christ died.

Perhaps you remember his words from 1 Corinthians 8:13. There, Paul wrote, "Therefore, if food makes my brother stumble, I will never eat meat, lest I make my brother stumble." Paul's concern here is far more than personal. He cares very little about his own reputation. The problem isn't that the Corinthians might think less of *him.* His concern is not merely for the *minister;* it's for the *ministry,* "so that no fault may be found with our ministry" (6:3).

When Paul lived among these people, his life was an open book to them. He spent eighteen months with them, and they had plenty of opportunities to examine his way of life. How could they now accuse him of fickleness or stubbornness? Paul could commend himself to the Corinthians in every way, something he would not do earlier (5:12). May God help and encourage us to conduct our service to Christ as His ambassadors so that we might be able to say the same!

As Paul writes about his ministry in 6:4–10, he uses a carefully crafted literary form. If you do not have your Bible open, you may want to open it now. (*Give group members time to find 6:4–10.*) Paul's ministry required "great endurance" (or "much patience"). Nine words flesh out what this phrase included: (1) afflictions; (2) hardships; (3) calamities (literally, "narrownesses"); (4) beatings; (5) imprisonments; (6) riots (or "insurrections"); (7) labors; (8) sleepless nights; and (9) hunger. Clearly, Paul had ample opportunity for exercising great endurance.

Following this is another list (v. 6) of qualities that characterized Paul's ministry: (1) purity; (2) knowledge; (3) patience (or "long suffering"); and (4) kindness.

This is followed (v. 7) by a set of four phrases descriptive of Paul's ministry: (1) [by] the Holy Spirit; (2) [by] genuine love; (3) by truthful speech; and (4) [by] the power of God.

Now come more descriptive phrases (v. 8), each preceded in Greek by the word *through* or *with* that is not always used in English translations: (1) "with weapons of righteousness for the right hand and for the left"; (2) "through honor and dishonor"; and (3) "through slander and praise."

This is followed (vv. 9–10) by seven contrasting units: (1) "treated as imposters, and yet are true"; (2) "unknown, and yet well-known"; (3) "dying, and behold, we live"; (4) "punished, and yet not killed"; (5) "sorrowful, yet always rejoicing"; (6) "poor, yet making many rich"; and (7) "having nothing, yet possessing everything."

In inspiring the apostle's words, the Holy Spirit uses all the abilities with which Paul was endowed, including literary skills, to bring His message to the Church in such a rich and pleasing way. The very structure of the text makes the point all the more emphatic: "We put no obstacle in anyone's way, so that no fault may be found with our ministry" (6:3).

Conclusion

How beautifully Paul presents the message of reconciliation through Christ! And more beautiful still is the message itself! The same beautiful message God entrusted to Paul and to his associates in ministry, including the Corinthians themselves, He has also entrusted to us. The war between you and your God has ended—at the cross. Jesus Christ has made peace possible. Live in that peace by His grace. And, relying on that same unfailing grace, carry that message of reconciliation into the world.

Concluding Activities

Speak a brief prayer, perhaps thanking God for having reconciled us all to Himself through Christ. Then make any necessary announcements and distribute study leaflet 5.

A Plea for Understanding

2 Corinthians 6:11–7:16

Preparing for the Session

Central Focus

Paul pleads with the Corinthians to open their hearts to him as he has opened his heart to them. The division between him and them is resolved by their repentance. Life in the Church today requires the same kind of openness and the same lifestyle of repentance for which Paul yearned and prayed in the Corinthian congregation.

Objectives

That participants, led by the Holy Spirit, will

1. know that a right relationship with fellow Christians results from a right relationship with God;
2. value Gospel-based Christian fellowship;
3. maintain a living relationship with God through His gifts of repentance and faith; and
4. maintain fellowship with other Christians through mutual forgiveness, love, and understanding.

Note for the small-group leaders: Lesson notes and other materials you will need begin on page 67.

For the Lecture Leader

Session Plan

Worship

Begin the session with the hymn printed in the study leaflet. Accompaniments are available in denominational hymnals, such as *Lutheran Service Book* or *Lutheran Worship* (refer to hymnal index). (Note: Concordia Publishing House has available *Every Voice a Song,* a 9-CD set of organ accompaniments for 180 hymns and liturgy. All the initial worship hymns in the LifeLight courses are included in this resource. It's especially helpful for mission congregations and small parishes. See the list of study resources on page 6.) Follow with the devotion.

Devotion

"For godly grief produces a repentance that leads to salvation without regret, whereas worldly grief produces death" (2 Corinthians 7:10).

If I were to ask you to name the greatest tragic figure in the Bible, who would it be? Almost certainly at least some of us would mention Judas Iscariot. Judas betrayed his Master, Jesus, with a kiss. Almost immediately he realized that what he had done was wrong. Judas even tried to make things right by returning the thirty pieces of silver to the temple authorities. Nothing worked. Judas was sorrowful. But instead of the "godly sorrow" that "brings repentance that leads to salvation," Judas looked only at his sin and at himself. He didn't look far enough. He needed to focus on the waiting arms of God. Instead, filled with sorrow and seeing no earthly way out, Judas sinned the ultimate sin. He despaired of God's help, rejected the Savior's forgiveness, and took his own life.

By way of contrast, think about Simon Peter. Peter knowingly denied his Lord in a cowardly, crude manner. His sin, too, drove him to sorrow. His pretensions, excuses, boasting, and self-help escapes all withered in an instant at Jesus' glance there in the courtyard of the high priest. Peter deserved death and hell just as surely as Judas did.

So why did Peter go on to serve Christ with the rest of his life while Judas lay in the Potters' Field? Peter saw Jesus—in His look in the courtyard, on the cross, and in the upper room on Easter evening.

Peter saw Jesus, and in Jesus Peter's helplessness, sinfulness, and unworthiness were removed. Jesus gave Peter new life. That's godly sorrow—the sorrow that "brings repentance and leads to salvation." Like Peter, we need always to look to the Savior, especially when we feel too unworthy and ashamed to look up. In Him we receive life and peace, mercy and forgiveness, newness and hope. God grant each of us that kind of repentant heart as long as we live here on earth!

Prayer

Forgiving Master, look not upon the times I have failed to look to You for help, but raise my eyes so that I may gaze upon Jesus only. Amen.

Lecture Presentation

Introduction

Have you ever found yourself the victim of misunderstanding—or, worse—of misrepresentation? If so, then you know the frustration of this situation. It is difficult to win back the hearts of former associates and friends, and to re-establish relationships, when you have to overcome wrong impressions. The task is all the more difficult when those who deliberately undermined the relationship in the first place are still at work, destroying your reputation.

That's the position in which Paul found himself in regard to the Corinthians. After he left Corinth, false teachers had wormed their way into the congregation and estranged the believers there from Paul. These false teachers had misrepresented him and maligned his motives. They had planted suspicion in the hearts of the Corinthians regarding Paul. Under the influence of these seducers, the Corinthians read into Paul's change in travel plans a sign of fickleness and stubbornness. Influenced by these smooth talkers, the Corinthians came to suspect that Paul fell short of their expectations of what an apostle should be. He was too much an earthen vessel.

This is the last section of the first major division of the letter, which deals with Paul's past relationships with the Corinthians. In it, Paul issues a plea for understanding that demonstrates his great love for his people and provides a model of the pastoral heart.

1 A Plea for Open Hearts (6:11–13)

In verse 11 Paul writes, "We have spoken freely to you, Corinthians; our heart is wide open." Paul protests that he is dealing openly with the Corinthians; he is being completely frank. He is speaking freely and holding nothing back. Paul didn't play games with those entrusted to his care. He did not tell them what he thought they *wanted* to hear, but rather, what they *needed* to hear. He never displayed anything other than the heart of a shepherd in his relationship with the Corinthians. The strain between Paul and the Corinthians was caused by the Corinthians, not by Paul.

But still, Paul complains that the Corinthians are withholding their affection from him. Literally, he says that their affection was being restricted, confined, cramped. This affection was not cramped by what Paul was doing or had done, but by the Corinthians themselves. The constraint in the relationship between Paul and the Corinthians came from their side, not Paul's.

How Paul feels this deprivation of their affections! Nevertheless, he continues to communicate with them from an open heart. Paul pleads with the Corinthians as a father might plead with his children. He pleads that they open up to him, that they open their hearts wide to him as he continues to do with them. Perhaps an awareness of their shabby treatment of Paul had led the Corinthians to think that Paul had shut them out of his own heart, that he no longer had any room for them there. Paul assures them that his heart is still open to them, and he urges them to make room in their hearts for him also.

Paul's plea is moving! It serves as an example of how we should deal with one another in the Church. We need not be afraid to let our true feelings show. We can, with Paul, dare to "wear our hearts on our sleeves." Paul was not too proud to take the first step in reconciliation, even though he was altogether in the right and those whom he addressed altogether in the wrong. We also can dare to take this courageous step of love. How many misunderstandings, how many long-standing divisions among Christians might have been avoided if someone had been willing to take the first step in addressing and healing differences! Perhaps we can do little to heal the divisions of the past. But we can resolve to do everything necessary on our part to keep divisions and lovelessness from arising in the future.

2 A Plea for Right Associations (6:14–7:1)

If Paul and the Corinthians were to be reunited, with their hearts open to one another, the Corinthians would have to get rid of some attitudes and behaviors with which Paul's detractors had infected the congregation. First among these was the spiritual partnership the believing Corinthians had tried to maintain with the unbelieving false teachers. For Christians and unbelievers to be (6:14) "unequally yoked" is surely a mismatch.

The phrase "unequally yoked" comes from the Old Testament. In Deuteronomy 22:10, God had commanded, "You shall not plow with an ox and a donkey together." To be sure, such a practice mismatched animals of differing size and strength. But the real mismatch from the viewpoint of Jewish law was linking a clean animal (one whose flesh could be eaten) with an unclean animal (meat forbidden by God). The ox was clean, and its meat could be used for food. The donkey was unclean.

It's beyond the scope of this lecture to explain God's purpose in declaring some animals "clean" and some animals "unclean" in the Old Testament ceremonial law. But the picture painted here is clear. Believers and unbelievers cannot be yoked together in spiritual partnership. Faith in Christ has made the believer spiritually clean before God; the unbeliever, without cleansing faith in Christ, is spiritually unclean. A spiritual partnership between them is a definite mismatch.

We need to note that by *unbelievers* Paul is not referring to *weak Christians;* he has already dealt with such relationships. Here it is Christian and unbeliever. Paul's detractors had given clear evidence that they worked as agents of Satan. For the believers in Corinth to join forces with such false teachers to advance the Gospel was unthinkable. The two would always pull in opposite directions.

Paul poses five questions to emphasize his point; each question requires that we answer with a resounding negative response (vv. 14–15):

- First he asks (v. 14), "What partnership has righteousness with lawlessness?" Obviously nothing.
- Second he asks, "What fellowship has light with darkness?" With the word *fellowship* here, Paul uses the word often translated "communion." Obviously, darkness cannot exist in light; light casts out darkness (John 1:5).
- Third Paul asks, "What accord has Christ with Belial?" As you learned in this week's study leaflet, *Belial* is a Hebrew term for Satan. Paul has already made the point that the Corinthians could not be partners with demons by participating in pagan worship (1 Corinthians 10:20).
- Fourth the apostle asks, "What portion does a believer share with an unbeliever?" What believers possess, unbelievers reject. How can they be yoked together? Will they not pull in opposite directions?
- Fifth and finally Paul asks, "What agreement has the temple of God with idols?" In Baptism, Christians become temples of the living God. How can idols live in God's dwelling? Remember Paul's point from his first letter to the church in Corinth?

"Do you not know that you are God's temple and that God's Spirit dwells in you?" (1 Corinthians 3:16).

"Or do you not know that your body is a temple of the Holy Spirit within you, whom you have from God? You are not your own, for you were bought with a price. So glorify God in your body" (1 Corinthians 6:19–20).

To drive his point home, Paul draws on a variety of quotations from the Old Testament (vv. 16–18). These words carry God's promises to be with His people, to be their God, and to live with them. He will be a Father to them, and they shall be His sons and daughters. For these reasons, His people are to be different, separate from the unclean people and things around them.

How we need to hear and heed Paul's words to the believers of ancient Corinth! Too often we Christians blend into the spiritual and moral landscape around us, living no differently from the world system in which we find ourselves. But like the Corinthian believers, we too are called by God to be different, to live as God's people who shine as lights in this dark world—because of *who* and *whose* we are. We might ask ourselves what implications Paul's comments have for the social ties we seek, the friendships we make, the business relationships we develop, the qualities we look for in a marriage partner, and in the other close relationships we form and nurture.

We should not fail to note that although in this chapter of his letter to Corinth Paul has quoted from Leviticus, Exodus, Isaiah, 2 Samuel, Hosea, Ezekiel, and Jeremiah, he begins this series of quotations (v. 16) with "as God said." The One who speaks all of these words is the Lord Almighty. What we have in the Sacred Scriptures is not, as some would have us believe, "the collective wisdom of the ages" or "the best that has come down from ancient spiritual giants," but the very Word of God.

Because we have such promises from God, Paul can call on those whom he addresses with the affectionate title (7:1), "beloved." But more meaningful still, because we have such promises from our Lord, Paul can invite all of us as God's people (v. 1) to "cleanse ourselves from every defilement of body and spirit." We can lead clean lives in both body and spirit. In this way we bring the fruit of Christian growth—godly living—to its goal.

Here is the reminder that Christian living is a constant process, a strenuous struggle that often includes many setbacks. Even so, we continue to strive, to "press on toward the goal for the prize of the upward call of God in Christ Jesus" (Philippians 3:14). Trusting in God's promises, we do not lose heart, we do not despair of our struggle with sin as we press on toward holiness. Nor are we so ready to jump on other Christians if they seem to lack our zeal or to live on our level of sanctification. Reverencing God, "fearing Him," as the apostle says, we receive freedom from having to compare ourselves with one another. We can concentrate instead on our own battle with sin and on God's promise that, as He works in us, we will continue to grow in the holiness both we and our Lord want in our lives, the holiness Jesus made possible when He exchanged our sinfulness for His righteousness (5:21).

3 A Plea for True Repentance (7:2–16)

So Paul once again (7:2) calls on his dear friends to make room for him, to receive him. He cites three reasons for them to do this. First, he has wronged no one; he has done none of them an injustice, either in his actions toward them or in his words written to them. Second, he has corrupted no one; he has brought no damaging influence on any one. Third, he has taken advantage of no one; he has not exploited them for his own purposes. Quite the opposite, he had taken no salary at all from them and had worked with his own hands to supply his needs and the needs of others with him.

Paul's goal has never been (v. 3) to condemn the Corinthians. What he has said before still stands; they were in his heart as ones with whom he had died and with whom he lived. The death has already taken place—both Paul and the Corinthians have died with Christ. The life they share is a continuing and a permanent process—they are alive with Christ forever. How could they be joined together more closely than by a common death and a common life?

So Paul writes frankly, in the plainest terms. But his frankness does not lead him to say something unpleasant. Rather, (v. 4) he takes great pride in them. He overflows with comfort for them. Though Paul had suffered great anxiety on account of the Corinthians, they also fill him with an immeasurable joy. In the Greek, Paul says that his joy over them "exceedingly exceeds its measure; it is present in abundance abundantly." (This may not be good English grammar, but expresses what Paul is saying.)

Paul's outburst of exhilaration comes from his joy in hearing that the people of Corinth had come to repentance. In 7:5 Paul is returning to the narrative he began in 2:13. Here he recounts in detail how he received this good news. When Paul had arrived at Macedonia from Troas, he still could find no rest for his anxiety concerning the Corinthians. There in Macedonia, he was afflicted at every turn. He faced "battles without"—the Gospel met opposition from unbelieving Jews and Gentiles. Perhaps Paul is thinking of some of the hardships he wrote about in 6:4–5. We don't know for sure because he does not identify the precise nature of his struggle. Nevertheless, he uses very strong language as he writes about this outward struggle.

Not only did Paul have to contend with opposition from without; he also had (v. 5) "fears within," fears about what was going on in Corinth. Paul was deeply concerned for his congregation.

At length, God allayed Paul's fears (v. 6). God, who comforts the downcast, comforted him by the coming of Titus. Paul took comfort in the very fact that Titus had finally arrived. But even more comforting was the news Titus brought with him and the way in which Titus had been encouraged by the response of the Corinthians. Titus told Paul of how the believers in Corinth anxiously awaited Paul's return to them, how they grieved and lamented over their sin, and how ready they were to extend a warm welcome to Paul. As a result of this message, Paul had all the more reason to rejoice.

For a time, Paul confesses (v. 8), he had had misgivings about the harsh letter he had sent to Corinth (the letter he mentions in 2:4—perhaps 1 Corinthians or perhaps another, severe letter that has not been preserved). Perhaps his letter had been too strong and had wounded the Corinthians too deeply. But now such misgivings had been set aside. While Paul regretted the case of incest and the way in which the Corinthians had dealt with it, he does not now regret the way he had taken the Corinthians to task in writing to them as he had, because it has produced the results (v. 9) that he (and the Lord) desired.

Paul's stern letter had caused the Corinthians to become sorry enough to repent (v. 10). It had caused the Corinthians grief—but the kind of grief God wants to see in sinners, a repentance that leads to salvation, with every cause of regret removed. There is another kind of grief, a grief caused by the world, a grief that leads to despair and to death. But this was not the grief that overtook the Corinthians; theirs was a good grief, a grief that led them to repentance and to life.

Grief by itself isn't enough. Sorrow over sin isn't enough. Such grief and sorrow may bring only death, not repentance that has life as its goal. That is why Paul now extols the kind of grief that God brought about among the Corinthians. Look at the results of this grief the apostle lists in verse 11. Each result is followed by one which is greater and even more important. Also note that Paul uses seven expressions—seven being the biblical number of completeness. See what godly sorrow has produced in the Corinthians: earnestness (at first the Corinthians were nonchalant about the case of incest; now they were dealing with it earnestly), eagerness to clear themselves, indignation (which replaced their lack of concern and attention to the matter), fear, longing (a true desire for Paul to come and help them in any of the ways in which they needed help), zeal, and finally, punishment (readiness to see justice done).

Taken together, these results point to one clear truth: the Corinthians had shown themselves to be pure with respect to the case; they are now clean with respect to it. They now have shown themselves to be true followers of Christ by the way they have taken care of the matter; they have cleared themselves with respect to it.

Now (v. 12) Paul reveals to them his underlying reason for writing to them as he had. His concern was not based chiefly on the concern he had for either the guilty party or the innocent victim. Of course, the guilty party had to be dealt with and brought to repentance. Of course, the innocent victim had to be given recompense for the wrong. But Paul had a larger goal in mind, one that had to do with the encouragement of the entire Corinthian congregation. The real purpose of Paul's letter was to have the Corinthians affirm their eagerness for Paul—not some kind of personal devotion, but the eagerness to hear and live the Gospel which Paul had proclaimed to them. Before God that is what truly mattered, that they received Paul's letter in such a way that they were turned to a renewed zeal for the Gospel. They had. Titus testified to that fact. And in that good news Paul was comforted.

Now Paul can bring this portion of his letter to a close. He has dealt with the past, with his authority and his ministry. The confidence that Paul had expressed to Titus regarding the Corinthians, his confidence that they would listen to God's Word of Law and Gospel, had turned out to be true. Paul had not boasted about them (v. 14) in vain. Titus, therefore, sends greetings to the Corinthians. His heart goes out as he remembers their obedience to the Gospel, the fear and trembling with which they received him as a messenger of the Word. Therefore, Paul rejoices (v. 16), because he has full confidence in his fellow Christians at Corinth.

Conclusion

What joy results in heaven and on earth among God's servants when God's people receive a word of rebuke in the right way, when such a rebuke clears away an offense that stands in the way of a relationship! We've all experienced relief and joy at a rebuke accepted, an apology given, a relationship put back on track.

Paul surely felt this sense of relief, for now the work of the Gospel could go forward once again in and from Corinth. Now that past problems are resolved, Paul and the Corinthians can go forward to present and future challenges. How is it with us? Is there a believer to whom you need to apologize? Are you ignoring or trying to justify a rift in the relationship between you and one of your brothers and sisters in Christ? You need not do that. Your Lord waits eagerly to give you the wisdom and the strength you need to begin to build a bridge from your side of the chasm. Why not ask Him for His grace to do just that now?

Concluding Activities

Speak a brief prayer, perhaps asking the Lord to remove any existing problems standing in the way of the Gospel in the lives of participants in the LifeLight assembly. Then make any necessary announcements and distribute study leaflet 6.

The Collection for the Saints in Jerusalem

2 Corinthians 8:1–9:15

Preparing for the Session

Central Focus

Christian giving, as a response of faith to God's grace in Christ, becomes a means by which God's grace flows abundantly through the life of the giver to others.

Objectives

That participants, led by the Holy Spirit, will

1. better understand the evangelical motive and character of Christian giving;
2. desire to grow in the grace of Christian giving; and
3. experience the privilege of Christian giving as a gift of God to the giver.

Note for the small-group leaders: Lesson notes and other materials you will need begin on page 70.

For the Lecture Leader

Session Plan

Worship

Begin the session with the hymn printed in the study leaflet. Accompaniments are available in denominational hymnals, such as *Lutheran Service Book* or *Lutheran Worship* (refer to hymnal index). (Note: Concordia Publishing House has available *Every Voice a Song*, a 9-CD set of organ accompaniments for 180 hymns and liturgy. All the initial worship hymns in the LifeLight courses are included in this resource. It's especially helpful for mission congregations and small parishes. See the list of study resources on page 6.) Follow with the devotion.

Devotion

"And this, not as we expected, but they gave themselves first to the Lord and then by the will of God to us. Accordingly, we urged Titus that as he had started, so he should complete among you this act of grace. But as you excel in everything—in faith, in speech, in knowledge, in all earnestness, and in our love for you—see that you excel in this act of grace also" (2 Corinthians 8:5–7).

The Bible has much to say about the grace of giving—from the collection for Solomon's temple to the sacrifice of the widow's mite to the parable of the talents.

The eighth and ninth chapters of 2 Corinthians deal with money, to be sure. Paul was concerned about the collection that had to be completed. But he was more concerned about the "grace of giving." The grace of giving is what made the temple collection so joyful, the widow's mite so lavish, and the talent that was buried so pitiful.

The grace of giving begins with the fact that we aren't the givers. God is! Paul wrote: "For you know the grace of our Lord Jesus Christ, that though He was rich, yet for your sake He became poor, so that you by His poverty might become rich" (2 Corinthians 8:9). God's giving of Himself is the source of the grace of giving, and He is the power behind all Christian giving.

In Christian giving, our money doesn't come first. Our hearts do. Did you catch what the Macedonian churches did first? "They gave themselves first to the Lord" (8:5). They made sure that the *main* thing was the main thing—not their money, but their hearts.

Then, knowing who the real Giver is, and knowing what the Lord wants first of all, the Corinthians would be ready to give to the collection "by the will of God."

In that spirit may the Lord lead us also to be His cheerful givers!

Prayer

Lord God, Giver of all good things, by the mercies of Christ use me as a means to bless others. Amen.

Lecture Presentation

Introduction

Fund-raising. Even hearing the words can cause some to cringe. Perhaps you also. Even when we advocate and enthusiastically support the cause for which funds are being raised, we may still regard the fund-raising itself as something distasteful that has to be done, a necessary chore.

Fund-raising, in this sense, has little to do with what Paul is referring to in the section we studied this week. The only connection between this kind of fund-raising and the grace of giving to which Paul refers is that in both cases money is collected. But the spirit and the attitude displayed in the process are far different.

As he writes to God's people, Paul refers to giving as an act of "grace" (8:7). This kind of giving is itself God's gift to the giver. God enables us to give; He provides both the motivation and the means. Furthermore, God blesses giving that is a response to His gift of grace to us in Christ. So God's grace floods the experience of giving from beginning to end. God enables and inspires our giving, and He blesses our giving. The more we tune in to Paul's concept of giving as a grace, the more our own offerings will be transformed into a blessing for us and for others.

1 Grace and the Collection (8:1)

The idea for the collection Paul talks about in the chapters we are studying this week went all the way back to the beginning years of the Christian Church—to the Council of Jerusalem reported in Acts 15:1–29. That council of Christian leaders was a watershed in the development and growth of the Christian Church because it settled the matter of how the Gospel was to be offered to the Gentiles. This council decided that a Gentile need not become a Jew in order to become a Christian.

The controversy that gave rise to the Council of Jerusalem could have resulted in two Christian churches, one for Jewish Christians and one for Gentile Christians. In fact, the struggle between these factions had come close to splitting the Church; that's why the Council of Jerusalem had met in the first place. Led by the Holy Spirit, the Council made it clear that there is one Church. What happens to one part of the Church affects the other parts. From that point in Church history onward, the conflict between the two factions stopped.

Later on, as Paul recounts for us in Galatians, the apostles came to a second understanding, a division of labor as it were. Peter and the other apostles would concentrate their ministry among the Jews, while Paul would concentrate his ministry among the Gentiles. At the time they agreed upon this way of organizing the ministry, they also agreed to continue to uphold the unity of the church. They agreed to love and support one another. Paul comments on their agreement in these words: "They asked us to remember the poor, the very thing I was eager to do" (Galatians 2:10).

As Paul wrote 2 Corinthians, that agreement was taking on a concrete expression; one part of the Church was in need. The believers in Jerusalem had encountered persecution and were suffering economically as a result. Because the Church is one body, the need of the Jerusalem Christians had become the need of the Gentile churches. Paul had called on the churches in Galatia, Macedonia, and Achaia to respond. At Corinth a beginning had been made in response to Paul's directions: "On the first day of every week, each of you is to put something aside and store it up, as he may prosper, so that when I come there will be no collecting" (1 Corinthians 16:2).

But the challenges that had been made to Paul's apostleship and authority had diverted the attention of the Corinthians from the collection. Perhaps some had charged that Paul was going to use the collection for his own purposes and that the poor in Jerusalem would never see any of it. By this point in his letter, Paul has settled the matter of his character and his call from the Lord. So now he urges the Corinthians to complete the collection they had started a year ago.

This section of the letter, in which Paul refocuses the attention of the Corinthians on the offering, is of special importance for us. It deals with one of the most sensitive aspects of the Christian life, Christian giving, in a thoroughly evangelical manner. Paul is not a fund-raiser, using his bag of professional gimmicks and tricks to separate the Corinthians from their cash. He is not some legalist who demands a certain amount because God requires it. He is not the huckster who promises rewards for gifts or threatens punishment for the lack of them. Paul is a pastor. His power lies in the Gospel.

Therefore, the key word as Paul discusses the offering is *grace.* Only the grace of God, His freely-given love for the sake of Jesus Christ, moves Christians to give God-pleasing offerings. Only those gifts that flow from grace please a gracious God.

2 Grace and the Macedonians (8:2–5)

Paul tells the Corinthians about how God's grace had moved Christians to respond with their offerings in the churches of Macedonia. The people of these churches suffered a most severe trial themselves (8:2), perhaps related to the conflicts Paul noted earlier (7:5). They were people of (8:2) "extreme poverty." The Greeks had two words for the poor. One refers to the person who owns no property, but who as a laborer lives from hand-to-mouth. The other word refers to someone who is dependent on the generosity of others. That second term is the one used here—and even this term is coupled with a descriptive word that means "to the depth," "bottomless," or "extreme." These people were really poor!

But their poverty became part of a surprising equation. Their poverty combined with an abundant joy and spilled over in a determination to give with great generosity (8:2b). They gave unconditionally. Their determination to give reflected their awareness that all Christians are of one mind and heart. The generosity Paul mentions here refers to more than the amount that was given; it refers to the spirit with which they gave their gift.

The Macedonians gave (v. 3) as much as they could—and more than they could. And they did this voluntarily. In fact, they begged earnestly (v. 4) for the privilege of sharing in this service to the saints. These Macedonians regarded the opportunity to take part in this offering as a gift in itself—a gift *they* were receiving. They regarded their sharing as Christian fellowship. They regarded this service to their fellow Christians as ministry. Notice here that the *contributors* did the begging, not those taking up the collection (v. 4). The conversation did not go, "please, give," but rather, "please, take this!"

That could happen only because the believers in Macedonia had given something else before they gave their money. First (v. 5), they gave *themselves* to the Lord and then to Paul and his partners who were serving the churches by the will of God. The Macedonians gave without reservation, without strings attached, unconditionally: first themselves to the Lord and to His apostle, then their gifts to the apostle for the benefit of the Lord's people.

3 Grace and the Corinthians (8:6–15)

Paul sets the example of the Macedonians before the Corinthians. He urged Titus to complete the project the Corinthians had started under Titus' leadership. This project is the collection Paul calls (v. 6) "this act of grace." As the Corinthians excelled in so many other things, so he urges them to excel also in "this act of grace."

Paul connects this grace with several other specific gifts in which the Corinthians excelled (v. 7). He begins with faith. Their faith had been threatened by the false teachers and by their own failure to deal promptly with their internal problems. But now their faith has been made firm again just as Paul said in chapter 1 (v. 24).

The second gift he lists is speech; the Corinthians confess with their mouths their faith in the Lord Jesus. They had once boasted of the gift of ecstatic speech (1 Corinthians 12–14). Now they use speech to proclaim the wonders of the One who had called them from darkness to light.

The third gift listed is knowledge. Not only did the Corinthians have a correct intellectual understanding of the faith, but they also understood the centrality of Christ for true knowledge (2:14; 4:6).

The fourth gift Paul lists is the Corinthians' earnestness. Unlike the situations that prompted Paul to write words of rebuke to them, the Corinthians were now not only willing, but eager to live according to the will of God.

Finally, Paul refers to their love for him. The relationship between the Corinthians and Paul had been shaky; they had been suspicious of Paul. Now this has changed. Love for Paul has been restored. And now, since the believers in Corinth excel in these five points, Paul sends Titus to them so that they might excel as well in the grace of giving for the relief of the saints in Jerusalem.

But notice that, while Paul urges and encourages, he does not command (v. 8). He holds before them the example of the Macedonians; the eagerness shown by the Macedonians becomes the opportunity for the Corinthians to test the genuineness of their own love. However, the example of the Macedonians is not to be the *reason* for the Corinthians to give, any more than the neediness of the people of Jerusalem is the reason to give. Needs become *opportunities* for giving. The giving of other Christians may set an encouraging *example.* But we do not give because there is a need or because others have responded. Christian giving flows neither from a sense of superiority nor a spirit of competition.

Rather, Christian giving flows from *grace.* Again, note that grace is the key word. Grace always takes us back to God. Paul reminds the Corinthians, "You know the grace of our Lord Jesus Christ" (v. 9). He was rich: God of God, Light of light, Very God of very God, King of kings and Lord of lords. Yet for our sake He became poor. (The Greek word for "poor" here is the same word used to describe the Macedonians in verse 2; it means that Christ became beggarly poor.) Paul described that self-imposed poverty of Christ in a letter written to the Christians of Philippi, one of the churches of Macedonia:

> Who, though He was in the form of God, did not count equality with God a thing to be grasped, but made Himself nothing, taking the form of a servant, being born in the likeness of men. And being found in human form, He humbled Himself by becoming obedient to the point of death, even death on a cross. (Philippians 2:6–8)

That's grace. And it is grace for us, so that we also through His poverty might be rich. With the Savior's grace in mind, Paul gives his opinion (v. 10). It's to the Corinthians' advantage that they complete what they began a year earlier, so that their initial willingness might be matched by their completion of the task. When that kind of willingness is present (v. 12), then God accepts the gift, not because of its size, but because of the spirit behind it. The smaller gift of a poor person is acceptable to God. The larger gift of a rich person is acceptable to God. God does not judge our gifts by their size but by the genuine willingness, the genuine response to God's grace the gift shows.

Paul does not want to burden the Corinthians by urging them to give more than others; rather, (vv. 13–14) it is a matter of equality. The apostle is not reminding the Corinthians that, while they are financially well off now, they may need the financial help of others in the future. Paul is not trying to make them see their gifts as some kind of insurance against future needs. No, Paul means that even in the present situation the Jerusalem church possesses an abundance of another kind (v. 14) to supply the present wants of the Corinthians.

When God's people give in the proper spirit, both givers and receivers are blessed. The poor in Jerusalem will be blessed in receiving financial relief from the Corinthians. But the Corinthians also will be blessed—by having an opportunity to express their love through their gift. Paul illustrates this truth in verse 15 as he refers to God's distribution of the manna to the Israelites in the wilderness. Just as the Lord saw to it that each Israelite received what was needed in the gathering of manna in the wilderness (Ex. 16:18), so He will use the offering to bless both the Jerusalem Christians and the Corinthian Christians.

4 Titus and His Companions (8:16–9:5)

Paul commends Titus and his companions to the Corinthians as well suited to carry out the details of the collection. God Himself has put the proper desire in the heart of Titus. Paul urged him to take the assignment, and Titus responded with enthusiasm.

Two men were to accompany Titus. Neither are identified, but both are described as highly qualified. As for the first companion, his previous service for the Gospel has earned high praise (v. 18) "among all the churches." This no doubt explains why the churches selected him for this task. Probably he was a Macedonian. Three men from that region are mentioned in Acts 20:4 as Paul's traveling companions: Sopater, Aristarchus, and Secundus. Whether Paul is referring to one of these, we do not know. The high reputation of this first companion of Titus would help to forestall any charges of financial impropriety. By his participation in the mission, this first companion would help to advance the other goals the churches wanted to accomplish in this offering (v. 19): honoring God and showing the eagerness of the Gentile Christians to help their Jewish Christian brothers and sisters. The way the project was carried out was to be honorable in the sight of God and men. There was to be no basis for gossip or criticism.

Paul does not identify Titus' second companion by name either, but he is described as one who had often proven his zeal for the Lord's work (v. 22). Evidently Paul had called upon him before, and he was never a disappointment. Also, he is described as eager and fully confident that the Corinthians are ready to carry out the collection that had been initiated a year ago.

So Paul commends the three men to the Corinthians. Titus is (v. 23) Paul's partner and his fellow worker. The other two are brothers in Christ, representatives of the churches, and an honor to Christ. For all these reasons, Paul urges the Corinthians (v. 24) to show them Christian love and to confirm the confidence Paul had expressed in them—not for his benefit, or for the benefit of the three messengers, but for the benefit of the churches themselves! Their response to the collection (v. 24) would demonstrate their unity and fellowship with the whole church.

Paul knows he really does not need to write the Corinthians about this service for the saints (9:1), for he knows of their eagerness to help. In fact, Paul has praised them to the Macedonians (v. 2). The Corinthians' enthusiasm had encouraged other churches to take part in the offering. Now, however, if the Corinthians do not come through on the collection, Paul's praise of them would sound hollow—in fact (v. 4), he would be embarrassed. Paul does not want that to happen. That is why he sent Titus and his two companions to finish the arrangements (v. 5) so that the collection would already be completed when the time came. It would be there waiting as a generous gift—not as something given grudgingly.

5 Grace and Freedom in Giving (9:6–15)

Note that Paul has emphasized the voluntary nature of the gift. And he does so once again beginning in 9:6. Each one must do as he has decided in his own mind (v. 7). The word Paul uses for "[make] up his mind" or "purposes" in this verse implies a free choice, one made without pressure—and, Paul adds, not reluctantly or under compulsion. He stresses the evangelical freedom each Christian has with regard to giving. Paul sums up his discussion with an adaptation of Proverbs 22:9: *The Lord loves a cheerful giver.* Christians give in response to God's grace, His own freely-given love in Christ. So Christians give cheerfully, remembering the words of Jesus, "It is more blessed to give than to receive" (Acts 20:35).

God's people know that (9:8) He is able to give His free gifts in such abundance that in *all* things and at *all* times we will have *all* we need so that we have the resources to do *every* good work. God takes such complete care of His people that they have everything they need to respond to His love. God makes it possible for us to know the joy of Christian giving by blessing us to the extent that we can exercise the privilege of giving He Himself has given us.

If we are to have the joy of Christian giving, then we need to remember why God blesses us as He does—not so we can hoard His gifts, nor so we can use everything He's given us for our own selfish pleasures or sense of security. Rather He wants us to have something to share with others. God deals with us in this respect like a Christian parent who gives his or her child a coin to place in the offering plate at church, to give to a charity, or to enable the child to help someone else. God is generous to us so we ourselves can show generosity to others.

Verse 6 explains a principle of giving familiar to gardeners and farmers. The Christian who sows sparingly, reaps sparingly; the Christian who sows bountifully, reaps bountifully. Crop yields depend, at least partly, on how much is planted. Christians know that God will supply the seed for sowing—He blesses us with something to give. We also know that He will provide a rich harvest to us as a result of our gifts.

And what is this harvest? If we give $10, can we know for sure we will receive $100 from God in return? You've heard claims like this from various Christian leaders and/or Christian ministries. Because you have read this far in 2 Corinthians and because you have studied chapters 8 and 9 closely, you know that the seed we sow is usually material—our gifts of money, the giving of our time, the use of our talents. But the harvest we reap is much grander.

In verse 13, Paul speaks of the harvest of thanksgiving and praise given to God by those who were blessed by the gifts the Corinthians gave. Back in 8:19, we read about the glory God received because of the generous hearts of the Corinthians. Giving that responds to God's grace in Christ, unconditionally, without coercion, with the single purpose of giving glory to a gracious Lord, produces thanksgiving and praise to God. Of course, the money or time or talents we give may also supply the physical needs of people—as when the gift of food results in nutrition and life.

Still, the harvest produced by our giving results in an even greater end: Those who receive our gifts, knowing their source and motivation, bubble over with many expressions of thanks to God. People will praise God for the faithfulness God has worked in us through the Gospel of Christ. They will praise God for the single-minded, devoted fellowship our Lord has enabled us to express toward them.

Paul describes the giving he has been encouraging as a sacred service (vv. 12–13). In fact, the Greek word he uses for "service" is the word from which we get our English word "liturgy." We might say that our giving is a liturgical response, an expression of worship, to the hearing of the Gospel. God gives first, and we give in response. What a beautiful idea, that our giving back to God what He has first given to us is an act of worship, an act of thanks and praise to Him!

Conclusion

All of this happens because of the surpassing grace of God in Christ Jesus. Only grace made the Corinthians

God's people. Only grace could open their hearts to respond to the needs of the Christians in Jerusalem. Only grace can do it for the Church today. And God's grace is surpassing; it goes beyond all that we can ask or think (Ephesians 3:20); it is always even more than we need.

In the face of all this, what other response can we offer than to say with Paul (v. 15), "Thanks be to God for His inexpressible gift"? God's gift is beyond telling. There are not words sufficient to describe what God has done for us in Jesus Christ. Language fails us. We can only respond with unspeakable awe as we thank Him.

Concluding Activities

Speak a brief prayer, accenting thanksgiving for God's wonderful grace. Then make any necessary announcements and distribute study leaflet 7.

Paul's Defense of His Ministry

2 Corinthians 10:1–18

Preparing for the Session

Central Focus

Paul defends his ministry against those who would judge him by worldly standards and commends his work to the Lord's approval.

Objectives

That participants, led by the Holy Spirit, will

1. know and affirm that the Christian ministry is not to be judged by worldly standards;
2. measure themselves by the standards of God's Word; and
3. boast in the Lord—that is, credit and praise God for what He is able to accomplish through us and others.

Note for the small-group leaders: Lesson notes and other materials you will need begin on page 73.

For the Lecture Leader

Session Plan

Worship

Begin the session with the hymn printed in the study leaflet. Accompaniments are available in denominational hymnals, such as *Lutheran Service Book* or *Lutheran Worship* (refer to hymnal index). (Note: Concordia Publishing House has available *Every Voice a Song*, a 9-CD set of organ accompaniments for 180 hymns and liturgy. All the initial worship hymns in the LifeLight courses are included in this resource. It's especially helpful for mission congregations and small parishes. See the list of study resources on page 6.) Follow with the devotion.

Devotion

"We destroy arguments and every lofty opinion raised against the knowledge of God, and take every thought captive to obey Christ" (2 Corinthians 10:5).

It must have been exceedingly hard for Paul. He was many miles removed from the Corinthians and unable to get there immediately. In the meantime, some in Corinth were hurting the cause of the Gospel by their actions and attacking Paul by their words. The apostle could only respond in writing and through those whom he sent to Corinth as his representatives.

How easy it would have been for Paul, like so many modern-day politicians who are running for office, to send a nasty and negative response. He could have filled his reply with half-truths and exaggerations. But Paul would have none of that. He saw what was at stake. Not him and his feelings, but the truth of the Gospel of His Lord and Savior. So Paul, empowered by God, took the high road. He made certain to "take every thought captive to obey Christ."

At times we also must deal with unscrupulous, unkind, unfair people—whether on the job, among acquaintances, or even right in our own family or church. How easy it would be to "[wage] war according to the flesh" (2 Corinthians 10:3). When we struggle with that temptation, the Holy Spirit helps us retain our perspective. An eternal perspective. We remember Christ—the One who for our sakes allowed Himself to be crushed down and abused. He died for *our* sins. And now His death frees us from our sins and enables us to deal with the sins of others head-on—in obedience to the love of Christ. Not ignoring the hurt. Not excusing the sin. But not taking personal revenge either. Relying on Christ and caring most of all about how the sinner can be brought to Him in repentance and faith, we receive courage and wisdom to act as our Savior Himself would act.

Prayer

Lord Jesus Christ, You defeated the sinful world, the devil, and my sinful flesh on Your cross. By Your Word and Spirit, enable me to do battle against these, Your enemies, to the glory of Your name. Amen.

Lecture Presentation

Introduction

We're about three quarters through 2 Corinthians, but several questions yet remain unanswered. The material we've read so far raised some of these questions. Paul now turns to address them as he prepares the Corinthian church for his next visit to Corinth. What are these questions? For example:

- Why, in the previous chapters, has Paul gone to such great lengths to explain that a change in his travel plans does not affect the unchangeable truth of the Gospel?
- Why does he insist that deferring his visit was to spare the Corinthians?
- Why did he have to defend the superiority of the new covenant over the old?
- Why were the Corinthians falling behind in the collection to which they had given such eager endorsement a year earlier?
- Why did Paul need to be so careful in explaining why he was sending Titus and two others to get the project moving again?

To such questions Paul now turns his attention.

Up to this point Paul has been open and conciliatory. However, he realizes that the enemies of the Gospel in Corinth must be exposed and condemned. Paul's adversaries must be met head-on, and their charges must be refuted for the sake of the Gospel of God's grace in Christ. Let's look at the charges these enemies have leveled at Paul.

1 The Charge: Paul Is a Pushover (10:1–6)

Paul begins the defense of his ministry emphatically and personally: "I, Paul, myself." Then he uses the word we have run across at least sixteen times in this letter: "I *beg* you." Paul makes his appeal on a basis that may not come across well to our ears; he appeals to the meekness and gentleness of Christ. Both "meekness" and "gentleness" as we use them today carry a handicap. To us, they may imply weakness or spinelessness—even gutlessness (to put it bluntly). We would have to say that most people today do not eagerly aspire to meekness—and often not even to gentleness. Our world does not seem to value these personal qualities.

Part of our problem lies in the fact that these English words no longer carry the meaning of the original Greek words the biblical writers, inspired by the Holy Spirit, had in mind when they chose them. The word translated "meekness" refers to an *inner attitude* of the heart that expresses itself in humility, courtesy, and consideration. "Gentleness" refers to an *outward conduct* toward people that is gracious and forebearing. Jesus describes Himself as gentle and humble in heart (Matthew 11:29).

Though outwardly soft, meekness and gentleness are inwardly strong, firm, and even tough. They are the hand of steel in a glove of velvet. King Jesus expressed these aspects of His ministry when He rode into Jerusalem "humble and mounted on a donkey" (Matthew 21:5). He displayed meekness and gentleness throughout His days on earth, a meekness and gentleness that reached their zenith at the cross. But we know that behind Jesus' meekness and gentleness lay a strength that did not crack beneath the extreme pressure of those days. These are the qualities in Jesus upon which Paul makes his appeal to the Corinthians.

Those who sought to undermine Paul's leadership in Corinth charged, "He puts on a bold front at a distance but in person, Paul is a pushover." In other words, they accused Paul of being a coward. For Paul to display any courage, they claimed, he has to be far away from those he is addressing. The Corinthians, of course, should have known better than to have listened to such charges. They should have dismissed them immediately. They knew Paul to be anything but a coward!

After all, they knew about the courage he had displayed at the Council of Jerusalem. That council took place shortly after Paul began his apostolic ministry. There he stood up to those who wanted to saddle Gentile Christian converts with obedience to the Jewish ceremonial law. Even before that council, Paul had taken on those same Jewish ceremonialists—legalists, really—at Antioch (Acts 15:2). Oh, Paul could be bold enough! Now he hopes it will not be necessary to show the Corinthians how bold he can be when he returns to Corinth and confronts those who have accused him of behaving by purely human standards.

Paul has a fight on his hands—even a war (v. 3). But the weapons he chooses to use are not those the world uses to fight its battles. Paul's weapons are spiritual weapons and, as such, have divine power to demolish spiritual strongholds. With these spiritual weapons, Paul smashes the clever but unsound and misleading reasoning the unbelieving world so loves to use. He demolishes every pretentious argument his opponents can set up against the right understanding of God's Word. Paul is no pushover.

But Paul is not out just to justify himself. He takes hold of his every thought and surrenders it to Christ. (The Greek expression Paul uses refers to taking prisoners of war.) Paul possessed a keen intellect, a sharp mind. He had been trained by the best teachers of his day, and he could take on the best thinkers in any intellectual argument. But Paul did not use his intellectual gifts and training for himself. He used them for Christ. He reserved them exclusively for service to Christ.

With his finely trained mind disciplined to use only the spiritual weapon of God's Word, Paul was ready to root out any disobedience he might find among those in the church at Corinth. Paul warns his opponents that they have something to dread when he returns. And as for the Corinthian believers, Paul expects them to develop and strengthen their own obedience to the apostolic Word while they wait for Paul to arrive.

We can learn a lot from Paul—just as he learned a lot from the meekness and gentleness of Christ. We can learn also to reject the weapons of the unbelieving world in our conflicts and to rely entirely upon the spiritual weapons God Himself provides. With these weapons, we know that we also will be able to overcome every assault of the devil and of those who knowingly or unknowingly serve the devil's goals. Like Paul we can face opposition honestly and directly, relying on the Lord and not on the underhanded strategies of this world.

2 The Charge: Paul Has No Authority (10:7–12)

Although the Holy Spirit was healing the church at Corinth, the false teachers still had an influence over the believers there. Paul urges the Corinthians to think through the claims of these teachers—to think them through again and with great care. "Take a good, hard look at what is staring you in the face in the influence of these false teachers," Paul is saying (v. 7). Look again!

Paul's opponents claimed, for instance, that they had come representing Christ—implying that Paul had not. Recall that one of the splinter groups referred to in 1 Corinthians claimed to "follow Christ," as if only they could make this claim (1 Corinthians 1:12). Look again at this arrogant claim, Paul urges the Corinthians. If someone is confident that he belongs to Christ (as if others—particularly Paul—did not), then such a person should consider again Paul's own connection with Christ. They should consider this: If Paul and his associates had not brought the Gospel to Corinth, would anyone there even now be a Christian? Give that some consideration, he urges! The false teachers in Corinth did not bring the Gospel to the Corinthians; Paul did.

If anyone claimed to belong to Christ, then certainly Paul could make this claim (v. 7). In actual fact, however, not only Paul but every genuine Christian can claim to belong to Christ, apostle or not. Looking more intently at the charges of the false teachers, we see an even more troubling question: May Paul claim the authority of Christ?

The apostle had already done that in his leadership at Corinth. The false teachers questioned his claim. How could he be an apostle, they had asked? Perhaps they brought up Paul's past as they tried to discredit him. Had he not persecuted the church? And everyone knew Paul had not been one of the Twelve. He had not been with Jesus during His earthly ministry. The false teachers at Corinth would not have been the first to question Paul's authority on these grounds; some in Galatia had stooped to these kinds of questions as well (Galatians 1:1).

But Paul reminds the Corinthians that his authority as an apostle was not something he had taken on himself; the Lord Jesus had given this authority to Paul. We remember how Jesus had stopped Paul (then known as Saul) and taken him prisoner on the road to Damascus. Saul was on his way to Damascus with another kind of authority altogether—authority from the chief priests at Jerusalem to arrest all who called on the name of Jesus (Acts 9:14). Jesus Himself had stripped Paul of that human authority and had given Paul another, opposite commission, with authority to do just the opposite of what he had set out to do. Paul had had authority to tear down the church; now he had been given Christ's own authority to build up the church.

The false teachers at Corinth were still trying to tear down, to destroy the faith that the Spirit had worked in the Corinthians by the Gospel. Paul *was* there to tear down too (v. 5)—but to tear down everything that stood in the way of their knowledge of God. Paul was not there to tear *them*—the Corinthians—down. He was there (v. 8) to build them up, to strengthen and preserve them in the true faith. That was his authority—the authority given to him by Jesus, who had taken him prisoner on the Damascus road. Of that authority Paul would not be ashamed. He would not yield it or give it up but tenaciously hold on to it and exercise it because the facts of how it had been given to him would bear him out.

But still other accusations came from the false teachers: Paul frightens us with his letter, they said (v. 9). His letters are weighty and strong, but his physical appearance is weak, and his speech is of no account. Such accusations ignored the fact that Paul's purpose was not to frighten the Corinthians. That what he writes is weighty and strong no one can deny. Every letter we today read from Paul's hand fits this description; every one is weighty and strong. Paul writes no piffle. But Paul's intention was never to frighten, but to build up.

True, Paul could and did write in blunt terms and use strong language. But was it true as well that in his personal speech he was waffling and weak (v. 10)? Paul's addresses preserved in the Book of Acts hardly fit such a description! His opponents at Corinth admitted the power and weight of Paul's letters—but only so they might attempt to present a belittling contrast with his personal presence and his speech. They claimed that these, at any rate, were weak and of no account, unimpressive and nothing to speak of. That was the claim.

Paul has an answer for that claim also: "Let such a person understand that what we say by letter when absent, we do when present" (v. 11). There are not two Pauls. Anyone who thinks Paul in person will be a pushover does not know Paul at all. Anyone who thinks he sounds tough only when he writes hasn't seen anything yet! Paul in person will put flesh and bones on his written words. Then, watch out!

In saying these things, Paul is not trying to stand on the same ground as his opponents, relying on worldly displays of power (v. 12). He is not resorting to their methods. Paul would not dare to classify or compare himself with those who commend themselves. He would not put himself in the same class or compare himself with those who never tire of praising themselves. Self-praise stinks. And these opponents of Paul at Corinth are masters of self-praise. Paul is bitingly sarcastic in referring to such self-inflating bluster. Those who practice it measure themselves by themselves and compare themselves with themselves. You can't lose that way—except in showing that you are not very intelligent.

Those who lead the Church today have authority also—but it is the authority of God's Word. When we attempt to base authority in the Church on things like "who I am" or "what I am" or "the way we have always done it" or on any ground other than the Word of God, we fall into trap of falsely-grounded authority and self-praise. Our only authority is and must remain the authority of God's Word. Empowered by the Spirit who inspired that Word, we also respond to that authority as the authority of God Himself, who deals with us through the Gospel.

3 The Charge: Paul's Boasting Knows No Limits (10:13–18)

The false teachers of Corinth presumed to evaluate Paul as an apostle by using worldly standards for measuring competence. Using such standards, however, were grossly inappropriate. Paul would not play this game. He would not measure himself by himself or compare himself with himself. Boasting "beyond limits" (v. 13) would both weaken what Paul said and say something different than he intended to say. Worldly standards are no measurement to use, Paul insists. Only a fool would do that. So much for the evaluation of Paul by those troublemakers in Corinth.

No, Paul would be measured by the standard that God has given. He would confine his boasting to the field God had assigned to him, a field that reached to and included the Corinthians. We know Paul as "the apostle to the Gentiles." That was the field God had assigned to him (Acts 9:15). He was not a parish pastor in the sense of a minister who is called to serve one parish or congregation in one specific place, who remains there to feed and tend this specific flock until he is called to serve another congregation in another place.

Rather, Paul was a planter, one who came to a place, proclaimed Jesus as Lord (usually first in the synagogue), gathered a following, installed pastors for the continuing care and encouragement of the congregation, and moved on.

Paul could boast that his work in Corinth followed the pattern God had assigned him. He was there first. The false teachers had not brought the Gospel to Corinth; they were intruders in the field assigned to Paul. Had Paul not come to Corinth with the Gospel first, then he might have gone too far in his boasting as he wrote of his authority among the Corinthians. But he had been the first to bring the Gospel to Corinth; therefore, his boasting would measure up to a proper standard. It was appropriate for an apostle, one who had been sent by the Lord as His ambassador, to bring them the Gospel.

Moreover, it was never Paul's practice to go where others had already gone with the Gospel. He did not boast in work done by others. He did not boast about work already done in another man's territory. That's precisely what his opponents had done in Corinth. That never had been Paul's practice, it was not his practice as he wrote to them, and it would not be his practice in the future.

Paul had plans for the future, plans which included the Corinthians. His hope was that, as their faith continued to grow, Paul's area of missionary activity would expand. He had every confidence that their faith would continue to grow. As that happened, the Corinthians would become Paul's partners in the work he had planned. Precisely how they would become involved Paul does not specify.

However, Paul's plans aligned perfectly with his customary pattern of ministry: He would preach the Gospel in the region beyond Corinth. What does Paul have in mind? It seems he is thinking of the region far to the west—Spain. Paul refers to this goal in his letter to the Romans (15:24). He planned to go to Rome, but since the church had already been planted there, he did not intend to work there. Instead, he planned to enlist the aid of the Romans also in bringing the Gospel to Spain (Romans 15:24, 28). The Corinthians, cleansed from the problems under which they had come close to losing it all, would have a part in bringing others to the faith. Great grace was at work among them.

Conclusion

Paul brings this discussion about boasting to a close. The words of Jeremiah apply to Corinth and to us in our day: "'But let him who boasts boast in this, that he understands and knows Me, that I am the LORD who practices steadfast love, justice, and righteousness in the earth. For in these things I delight,' declares the LORD" (Jeremiah 9:24).

It is not the one who commends himself who is approved. People who know that they were "by nature sinful and unclean," who know that they did not come to believe in Jesus Christ "by their own reason or strength," who know that they are what they are only by the grace of God, know that well. The one who is approved is the one whom the Lord commends. Paul knew what that meant for his ministry. Paul's comment in 1 Thessalonians brings us to an appropriate conclusion here also: "But just as we have been approved by God to be entrusted with the gospel, so we speak, not to please man, but to please God who tests our hearts. For we never came with words of flattery, as you know, nor with a pretext for greed—God is witness. Nor did we seek glory from people, whether from you or from others" (1 Thessalonians 2:4–6). We are to know that too. The one who is approved is the one whom the Lord commends. Whatever we are able to accomplish is by grace alone.

Concluding Activities

Close with a brief prayer, perhaps thanking God for His grace in bringing the Gospel to us and asking God to help us share the Gospel with others. Then make any necessary announcements and distribute study leaflet 8.

Paul's "Foolish" Boasting

2 Corinthians 11:1–12:21

Preparing for the Session

Central Focus

Though reluctant, Paul feels driven to boast, to speak about himself, his accomplishments, and his weaknesses so he might defend the ministry the Lord had given him against the false charges of his opponents in Corinth.

Objectives

That participants, led by the Holy Spirit, will

1. understand more about Paul's personal career as an apostle through the information he provides as he "boasts";
2. be encouraged by the lesson God taught Paul through his thorn in the flesh—that God's grace is sufficient for us as we go about the tasks He gives to us; and
3. give glory and honor to God for what He accomplishes through us.

Note for the small-group leaders: Lesson notes and other materials you will need begin on page 76.

For the Lecture Leader

Session Plan

Worship

Begin the session with the hymn printed in the study leaflet. Accompaniments are available in denominational hymnals, such as *Lutheran Service Book* or *Lutheran Worship* (refer to hymnal index). (Note: Concordia Publishing House has available *Every Voice a Song,* a 9-CD set of organ accompaniments for 180 hymns and liturgy. All the initial worship hymns in the LifeLight courses are included in this resource. It's especially helpful for mission congregations and small parishes. See the list of study resources on page 6.) Follow with the devotion.

Devotion

"So to keep me from being too elated by the surpassing greatness of the revelations, a thorn was given me in the flesh, a messenger of Satan to harass me, to keep me from being too elated. Three times I pleaded with the Lord about this, that it should leave me. But he said to me, 'My grace is sufficient for you, for my power is made perfect in weakness.' Therefore I will boast all the more gladly of my weaknesses, so that the power of Christ may rest upon me" (2 Corinthians 12:7–9).

We do not know what Paul's "thorn in the flesh" was. Whatever the "thorn" was, it was something that Paul didn't want. He describes it as a "messenger of Satan to harass me." Three times he pleaded with the Lord to remove this thorn. The Lord answered Paul's prayer. His answer was "No."

Sometimes we Christians delude ourselves by thinking that our lives should be free of troubles. As God's children, we shouldn't have to put up with small burrs and thistles, let alone sharp thorns that come from Satan. However, we live in a sinful world where sickness, tragedy, and even death abound. Like it or not, we'll not escape life's thorns any more than Paul could.

That doesn't mean we can't or shouldn't pray mightily, asking the Lord to remove them. Paul certainly did, and we can too. But Paul also knew who was Lord and who wasn't. The third time Paul prayed, the Lord answered, "My grace is sufficient for you, Paul." At that point, Paul knew that the Lord's will was being done, and he entrusted himself to that will.

Paul also seemed to know that his weakness was no accident. The Lord demonstrated His power in Paul's case through Paul's weakness, and Paul could rejoice in that.

We can always trust our Lord to give us precisely what we need. We can lean on Him in times of sickness and health, sorrow and joy because He gives us Himself. In the midst of our own personal weaknesses, we know that Christ's power rests on us as surely as it rested on the apostle Paul. And we can praise our Savior for that strength ever at work in our lives.

Prayer

Gracious Father, in the midst of my many weaknesses, demonstrate the strength of Your love for me through Christ Jesus, our Lord. Amen.

Lecture Presentation

Introduction

In many respects this section of the letter is the most fascinating of all of it. Here we find Paul engaged in doing something that goes against everything he thought an apostle should be. We find Paul boasting. Now boasting was not something that Paul took to. But if some foolish boasting was necessary to silence the bragging of those false teachers who had come to Corinth, wormed their way into a position of influence in the congregation there, and boasted of their own authority as they criticized and opposed Paul, then Paul could play the boasting game as well as any. He admits that it is foolish. But sometimes it takes a dash of foolishness to make a point.

As he proceeds to boast, Paul becomes autobiographical. We learn something about the joys and sorrows in his ministry. But most of all, we see the love a pastor can have for God's people, the love of a pastor like Paul who will most gladly spend and be spent for the souls entrusted to his care.

1 Paul and the False Apostles (11:1–15)

Paul begins hesitantly and with an apology: "I wish you would bear with me in a little foolishness." These are hardly the words of a died-in-the-wool, well-practiced braggart. But his tentative start soon gives way to a greater certainty: "For you gladly bear with fools," he writes. Paul has a special relationship with these Corinthians and that relationship will cause them to go along with him in this foolish exercise of his. Paul is jealous for the believers in Corinth with a godly jealousy.

Paul almost immediately turns to a word picture. He depicts himself as one who has arranged a marriage. As their spiritual father, Paul had promised the Corinthians as a bride to Christ, and he had hoped to present them to Him just as a proud father would present a pure virgin to her one husband. (In Paul's day, parents commonly had such a role in the lives of their children.) Yet, Paul fears that this will not turn out to be the case. He fears that, just as Eve was utterly deceived by the serpent's cunning, the Corinthians will be led astray from their singleness of purpose and pure devotion to Christ.

Paul's fears were not out of touch with reality. In fact, Paul had every reason for his fear. The Corinthians had already put up with the false teachers, and they had done so in grand style. Their eager acceptance of these false teachers is all the more remarkable in the light of what these men taught. They grossly distorted the faith that Paul had brought to Corinth. They spoke of Jesus, the Spirit, and the Gospel—but they used these familiar terms to mask teachings that were far different from those the Corinthians had heard from Paul.

The Jesus of these false teachers was not that same Savior Paul proclaimed. The spirit the false teachers served was not that same Holy Spirit who enabled and worked through Paul. The gospel they preached was not that same Gospel of God's free grace for all for Christ's sake that Paul preached. So Paul's fears were certainly justified.

The false teachers of Corinth claimed to be far superior to Paul. However, Paul suggests, let's look at the facts. How do these slick, smooth-talking charlatans stack up to the apostle Paul and the message he proclaimed? Paul declares that he is not in the least inferior to these "super-apostles" (v. 5). True, Paul admits, I am an amateur—not a specialist, but only a layman—when it comes to training and expertise in public speaking. Paul may have been no match for the oratorical skills of these braggarts, but he had it all over them in spiritual knowledge. The Corinthians knew this; it had been made perfectly clear to them in every way.

Still, there were those who objected to Paul. In their opinion, Paul had not been altogether professional in the way he conducted himself. According to accepted professional procedures in the Greek world at that time, teachers were compensated for their work. In fact, the better the teacher, the more he earned. Salary was a kind of professional measuring stick. The greater the pay, the greater the regard in which teachers would be held by their followers and by society generally. The world still regards public figures in this way; personal earnings are still considered a measure of worth and effectiveness. By this measure, Paul was a manifest failure. He took no payment in Corinth, and this, it was charged, proved that his teaching was worthless.

Paul responded by asking (v. 7): "Or did I commit a sin in humbling myself so that you might be exalted?" Paul had proclaimed and taught the Gospel freely, without payment, as a gift. More than this, Paul even took from other churches to serve the Corinthians; he accepted support from others so he might serve them (v. 9). Paul had kept himself from being a financial burden to the Corinthians—and he pledges that he will continue to do so. Paul bore Christ's own truth. And for the sake of that truth, he would not be silenced, not until the truth of the Gospel had been heard throughout Achaia (southern Greece). And why wouldn't he stop this boasting of how he had served the Corinthians without pay? Was it because Paul didn't love the Corinthians and wanted to embarrass them (vv. 10–11)? God knows otherwise.

No, Paul will *not* shut up. He will continue his practices of preaching without pay so he might cut the ground out from under the feet of those who boast that they are his equals—and better than his equals (v. 12). He will continue to proclaim and teach the Gospel without charge. In doing this, Paul will expose his opponents for what they are: false apostles, dishonest, fraudulent workmen, masquerading as apostles of Christ (vv. 13–15).

The Corinthians should not have been surprised any more than we should be that false teachers—false apostles—arise and try to mislead many. Satan often disguises himself as an angel of light. So no wonder that Satan's servants masquerade as servants of righteousness when they are anything but that. What else should anyone expect? But we, like the Corinthians before us, need not fret. In the end, these enemies of the Gospel will get what their actions deserve. For a while the false apostles seem to carry the day. They put on a great show. They drip with false piety. They parade their credentials. But the Lord will have the last word. They will not be able to stand in His judgment. But Christ's true apostle—Paul—will, God knows! And those who believe the Word proclaimed by Paul will be able to say with him: "The truth of Christ is in me."

2 Paul's Suffering as an Apostle (11:16–33)

But Paul is not finished with his boasting yet. Paul is no foolish braggart, but since the Corinthians seem to regard him as a fool, then he will act like a fool and do a little more boasting (v. 16). Paul doesn't really enjoy this role that has been thrust upon him. He is uncomfortable with it and acknowledges (v. 17) that this is not the way the Lord would speak. But since the false teachers have chosen to contend with him on the level of the world, Paul will take them on on that ground. And surely Paul's foolish boasting shouldn't bother the Corinthians (vv. 18–19). They're so wise that they gladly put up with fools. (Paul's words here drip with sarcasm.)

He continues in verse 20, saying in essence, "You put up with it when someone enslaves you again by taking away the freedom you have in the Gospel of Christ, when they exploit you by taking such exorbitant salaries, when they take advantage of you and lord it over you, when they push themselves forward and act so presumptuously with you, or when they slap you in the face with their charges against the Gospel that you had received." The Corinthians needed to hear—loud and clear—the truth about their relationship with the false teachers. And so Paul lays it out for them. The false teachers had treated them most shabbily, but the Corinthians took it without complaint, smiling all the while.

Paul confesses (v. 21) that he had no stomach for such overbearing, arrogant behavior. He could not personally pull it off. "We were too weak for that!" he exclaims. But since the Corinthians delight in foolish boasting, Paul will dish out even more of it.

The false teachers boasted of credentials they didn't really have. They dared to parade their stuff. Since they had set the pace, then Paul the fool could keep up. The false teachers were Jews and proud of it. They were Hebrews, Israelites, and descendants of Abraham. Paul can match each boast: "So am I," he declares (v. 22). In fact, Paul could go them one better. Paul's Jewish parentage was without question, and his upbringing had been strictly by the book, strictly according to the letter of the Law. He had been thoroughly trained in the Law under Gamaliel (Acts 22:3), the most honored rabbi of the first century. As a young man, Paul had become a Pharisee and had distinguished himself by his zealous activity in that strict Jewish sect, including his persecution of Christians. Paul's pursuit of a legalistic righteousness had been faultless (Philippians 3:4–6).

Paul was not only a better Jew, he is a better servant of Christ (v. 23). (Paul admits he is speaking as though he were out of his mind.) He has worked much harder, been in prison more frequently, been flogged more severely, and has been exposed to death again and again. And the evidence? Paul offers details in verses 23–25. Five times Jewish persecutors had laid on him the forty lashes minus one. And, beyond that, Paul had received three beatings with rods at the hands of Roman authorities, although as a Roman citizen Paul was legally protected from such punishment (Acts 16:37–39; 22:25–29). At Lystra he had been stoned (Acts 14:19). Three times he was shipwrecked (Acts 27:1–44); he had spent a night and a day in the open sea. All of this happened because he was a minister of Christ.

He had been constantly on the move, going from place to place to preach the Gospel. He faced eight kinds of dangers. The first two are from rivers and bandits. The second two indicate the source—from his own countrymen and from Gentiles. The next three indicate the places where Paul faced dangers—the city, the country, the sea. Finally, he had had to contend with false brothers, the most unexpected source (vv. 26–27). Paul experienced exhausting labor and hardship. With four phrases, he paints the picture: in sleeplessness often, in hunger and thirst, in fastings often, in cold and nakedness. And as if all this were not enough, he had the anxious care of a pastor concerned about all the congregations the Lord had entrusted to him (v. 28).

But there is even more to boast about. Paul can boast about his weakness (vv. 31–32). Paul has news for those who think the ministry of the Gospel is all honor and glory. In Damascus the governor had the city guarded so he might hem Paul in and arrest him. Paul escaped by being lowered in a basket from a window in the wall and, in this way, he slipped through the governor's hands (Acts 9:23–25). Paul's escape was no heroic escapade. His ministry began with his being sneaked out of town in the dead of night! Not much glory in that!

But if Paul has to boast, he will boast of such personal weakness. Paul's boasting, after all, was not to elevate himself but to elevate the Lord whose servant he was and in whose service he had done all these things. What encouragement for us to give ourselves to the Lord's service!

3 Paul's Visions and Revelations (12:1–6)

Yet it is boasting the Corinthians seem to want! So Paul will oblige them, even though he sees nothing to be gained by it. He will go on to visions and revelations he had experienced. Paul speaks about "a man" who experienced this vision as though it were someone other than himself. But the reference to "me" in verse 7 suggests that the person he tells about was indeed Paul himself. The phrase *third heaven* refers to the eternal, glorious home of God, the angels, and the saints—heaven itself. Paul uses the word *third* to distinguish it from the sky, the "heavens" above the earth and space of this creation.

The experience Paul describes goes beyond even his ability to understand or grasp. He does not know whether he was in the body or out of it. He heard things that are inexpressible. The human voice is incapable of relating what he heard. If one is to boast, then here is room for boasting. Here is an experience used by the Lord to strengthen Paul for his task. In boasting of this he would no longer be playing the fool. But God gave this experience to Paul for Paul's benefit. He was not to focus on it or use it to draw undue attention to himself. Paul did not want to become puffed up about himself because of something that the Lord, in grace, had permitted him to experience.

4 Paul's Thorn in the Flesh (12:7–10)

To keep Paul from being unduly elated, even conceited, because of the surpassingly great revelations, the Lord allowed Paul to experience "a thorn . . . in the flesh, a messenger of Satan," to torment him. No one now knows what that thorn was, and Paul does not tell us. As you might imagine, many have had a field day guessing at what it might have been. Epilepsy. Hysteria. Depression. Headaches and eye trouble. Malaria. Leprosy. Speech impediments. All of these ideas have had their proponents. Perhaps Paul does not define it more specifically so that we ourselves can insert our own personal "thorn" there as we read about it and about Paul's frustration with how it hampered his work for the Lord Jesus.

What we do know is how Paul responded to this thorn in the flesh. Three times (repeatedly) he pleaded with the Lord to take it away. And the Lord answered Paul's prayer. How Paul received this answer we do not know. But the Lord's answer was direct and final. The Lord assured Paul, "My grace is sufficient for you" (v. 9). Paul might have argued that the thorn kept him from fulfilling his apostolic task of preaching the Gospel and that its removal would have advanced the Gospel. But the Lord's work did not depend on Paul's strength or ability. God's grace alone would get the Gospel out into the world. God in His grace had chosen Paul. God's grace would be enough to supply Paul's every need. The power of grace is made perfect in weakness. Realizing that, Paul all the more gladly boasted of his weaknesses so that the power of Christ might overshadow him, might spread its tent over him.

Realizing this grace and relying on it, Paul could delight in his weaknesses and in the insults, hardships, persecutions, and difficulties he endured for the sake of Christ (v. 10). For now Paul realized that when he is weak—when he can no longer depend on himself—

then he is truly strong, for then he depends entirely upon God. And God is completely dependable.

5 Paul's Concern for the Corinthians (12:11–21)

Paul knows he has been playing a fool's game with his boasting. But the Corinthians forced him to it. In no way is Paul inferior to the "super-apostles." The marks of a true apostle—signs, wonders, and miracles—had been demonstrated repeatedly by Paul in Corinth. Paul does not mention details here. But his ministry at Ephesus gives us some idea. About that ministry, Acts 19:11–12 reports, "And God was doing extraordinary miracles by the hands of Paul, so that even handkerchiefs or aprons that had touched his skin were carried away to the sick, and their diseases left them and the evil spirits came out of them."

Having witnessed testifying miracles like these, how could the Corinthians possibly claim that they had received inferior treatment from Paul? Oh, Paul remembers one thing: he did not burden them by taking a salary from them. Sorry about that! "Forgive me this wrong," Paul begs (v. 13), as he begins to move his defense of himself into the next phase of his letter—his plans to visit the church in Corinth.

This visit will be his third (v. 14). And, as before, he does not intend to be a burden to them this time. He does not want their possessions; he wants *them.* After all, children are not obliged to save up for their parents; it's the other way around. Paul will most gladly spend and be completely spent for their souls. Because Paul loves the Corinthians more, should they love him less? But even if they should, still he will not be a burden to them.

In making that assertion, Paul brings up another charge that had been made against him: that he is an unscrupulous trickster, someone who will do anything to achieve his aim (v. 16). His opponents claimed that Paul's modesty was artificial and, in reality, only an evil trick. They charged that Paul caught the Corinthians by trickery, that he deceived them. Well, if that were true, Paul argues, then there must be some evidence. "Did I take advantage of you through any of those whom I sent you? . . . Did Titus take advantage of you? Did we not take the same steps?" No one could point to a single act of Paul or of any of his representatives that would indicate that Paul wanted money from the Corinthians for his personal use. The charges were clearly false.

In all of this, Paul has not been primarily concerned to defend himself to the Corinthians (v. 19). More is at stake than merely Paul's personal honor. Rather, God's honor is at stake. In the presence of God and as someone who is in Christ, Paul makes his case to build up the Corinthians, to strengthen them as God's people.

Paul knows Corinth well. He knows the damage that the false apostles had done. He knows that everything in the church there is not as it ought to be. And what he knows worries Paul (v. 20). He mentions three specific concerns.

First, he fears that perhaps when he comes he will not find the Corinthian believers as he wants them to be, and they will not find him as they want him to be. If all the work he has done among the Corinthians has not brought about the results he desires, they will not be pleased with the Paul who will confront them.

Secondly, Paul fears that perhaps there will be some behavior that needs correction. He lists eight items. The first two are singular: quarreling and jealousy. The next six are plural, and can be translated (v. 20) as *acts of* outbursts of anger, selfish ambition, backbiting, gossip, self-importance, and disturbance. It's worth noting that all of the behaviors he mentions grow out of the kind of disunity and cliquishness that has been such a problem at Corinth. If true repentance has not taken place, then their progress has been more apparent than real.

Finally, Paul fears—and there is no "perhaps" to soften the language—that God may humble him and he will be grieved over many who had sinned earlier and had not repented of the impurity (the immorality), sexual sin (fornication), and debauchery in which they have indulged (v. 21).

Paul knew the Corinthians and their sins. He knew the cavalier attitude with which they had met the case of incest among them at first. Even though the case had now been settled, not all had forgiven freely, and the brother who had fallen into this sin was in danger of being overwhelmed by excessive sorrow (2:6–7). The Corinthians had been careless with respect to the pagan festivities and questions about their participation (1 Corinthians 8 and 9). They had not resolved all the questions about sexual behavior (1 Corinthians 6:12–20). It is no wonder Paul expresses his fears as he contemplates his visit to Corinth.

He has such high hopes, such great expectations regarding these, his children in the faith. But what if not all is well? It is the pastor in Paul that causes him to express his fears in such an open and honest way. After all, he is writing to his dear friends, to his beloved.

Conclusion

The two chapters we have just studied have given us an intimate and revealing glimpse into the heart and life of the apostle Paul. He has exposed his soul. He has boasted of his accomplishments (a foolhardy venture, by his own admission). And he has boasted more so of his weaknesses. All of this has exposed a pastor who passionately loves the people whom God has entrusted to him, a pastor who loves them enough to hold nothing back from them.

We thank God for giving His church such a pastor, such an apostle in Paul. And we continue to thank Him, too, for those who work among us in the same task that Paul had—spreading the Gospel of our Lord Jesus. We pray that God's grace and power will be poured out upon them. We pray that they would, by grace, always have the love and courage they need to confront us with our sins and to comfort us with the Good News that God freely forgives us in Jesus. And we ask that that same grace would rest on us as we serve others in Christ's name, realizing that the strength to do so must come—always and only—from God's grace at work in us despite our weakness. God grant all these things for Jesus' sake!

Concluding Activities

Conclude the session with a brief prayer, perhaps asking that each of you would be more willing to entrust yourselves to God's grace as your greatest strength. Then make any necessary announcements and distribute study leaflet 9.

Paul's Impending Visit to Corinth

2 Corinthians 13:1–14

Preparing for the Session

Central Focus

Paul is now ready to make his long-delayed visit to Corinth. As he prepares for this visit, he speaks a final warning as well as assurance and love for the repentant.

Objectives

That participants, led by the Holy Spirit, will

1. rejoice that God's ultimate intention is to forgive and restore us when we sin so we might receive His grace and be saved;
2. regard the Gospel and those who proclaim it as having the power of God; and
3. examine themselves daily so that they remain in the faith and exhibit that faith in love toward others.

Note for the small-group leaders: Lesson notes and other materials you will need begin on page 79.

For the Lecture Leader

Session Plan

Worship

Begin the session with the hymn printed in the study leaflet. Accompaniments are available in denominational hymnals, such as *Lutheran Service Book* or *Lutheran Worship* (refer to hymnal index). (Note: Concordia Publishing House has available *Every Voice a Song*, a 9-CD set of organ accompaniments for 180 hymns and liturgy. All the initial worship hymns in the LifeLight courses are included in this resource. It's especially helpful for mission congregations and small parishes. See the list of study resources on page 6.) Follow with the devotion.

Devotion

"The grace of the Lord Jesus Christ and the love of God and the fellowship of the Holy Spirit be with you all" (2 Corinthians 13:14).

It is not surprising at all that Paul would end this letter with the words of a blessing that names the triune God.

That's the way he began the letter (1:2). That's the way that Paul proceeds throughout the letter by naming the name:

- when he had to explain his change of plans (1:23);
- when he asked the Corinthians to be forgiving toward a repentant sinner (2:10);
- when he discussed the heart of his ministry (4:5) and the heart of the Gospel (5:19);
- when he wrote about giving a special offering (8:9);
- when he had to defend himself against the accusations of false apostles (11:31); and
- when he expressed his deep concern for the believers in Corinth (12:19).

For many of us, our new life in Christ began with our being named by that name—as the waters of Holy Baptism were applied to us and the name of the Father and of the Son and of the Holy Spirit were spoken over us and tied to our personal names forever.

That's the way that our lives proceed, for we live and continue to grow as Christians by the grace of our merciful Savior who gives us everything we need for life and salvation. We rejoice in the Father who loves us with an eternal love and delights to call us His children. We celebrate the sanctifying power of the Holy Spirit who, as Luther expressed it in his explanation of the Third Article of the Apostles' Creed, "calls, gathers, enlightens, and sanctifies" us and keeps us in the true faith and in fellowship with Him and with others whom He also has called to faith.

With this lesson, we come to the close of this book, 2 Corinthians, and to the close of this study. From beginning to end *it* and *we* have been marked by the blessing of the Triune God. How blessed we are!

Prayer

Gracious God—Father, Son, and Holy Spirit—thank

You for naming me with Your name in Holy Baptism and adopting me as Your child forever. Amen.

Lecture Presentation

Introduction

The practiced letter-reader, the practiced conversationalist, the practiced sermon-listener—all can tell when the letter, the conversation, the sermon is drawing to a close. Tell-tale phrases provide the clue:

- Well, I can't think of anything else new.
- I guess I've bent your ear long enough.
- And finally . . .

As Paul draws 2 Corinthians to a close, we pick up on the same kinds of clues:

- This will be my third visit to you . . .
- Finally, brothers . . .

In this letter, Paul has opened his heart and his ministry to the Corinthians. He has written of his great anxiety and of how that anxiety was relieved by good news brought by Titus. He has boasted of his achievements—and of his weaknesses—to underline the all-surpassing grace and greatness of God. He has pleaded and threatened. It is now time to say good-bye, but even his good-bye expresses his hope and anticipation.

1 A Call for Repentance (13:1–4)

Paul begins the final section of this letter by noting again that the coming visit will be his third to them. The fact that his visit had been delayed set the tongues of the false teachers wagging. The situation is like that described in 1 Corinthians: "Some are arrogant, as though I were not coming to you. But I will come to you very soon, if the Lord wills, and I will find out not the talk of these arrogant people, but their power. For the kingdom of God does not consist in talk but in power. What do you wish? Shall I come to you with a rod, or with love and in a spirit of gentleness?" (1 Corinthians 4:18–21).

Paul has already mentioned the inclination of the Corinthian believers to backbiting and gossip (12:20). So he reminds them (13:1) of the command laid down in the Scripture regarding fair dealing with those trapped in sin. "Every charge must be established by the evidence of two or three witnesses." Paul is referring to Deuteronomy 19:15: "A single witness shall not suffice against a person for any crime or for any wrong in connection with any offense that he has committed. Only on the evidence of two witnesses or three witnesses shall a charge be established." If the person were guilty and sentenced to death, the hands of the witnesses had to be the first to carry out the execution (Deuteronomy 17:7). God will not permit anyone to be dealt with on the basis of rumor.

So Paul repeats the warning he had given in person on his second visit. What he had already told those who continued in their former sins and all the rest when he was with them, he tells them again before he comes (13:2). He will not spare them; he will not be lenient. He will not be a pushover. Instead, he will take the necessary steps for bringing about obedience to God's Word. Paul knew that the sin of one member affected all members (1 Corinthians 12:26). Paul will deal fairly and evangelically; he will continue to exercise patience and love. But a refusal to repent must finally be dealt with firmly and decisively. If necessary, Paul will deal with the unrepentant sinner in a manner that will remove all doubt. He will not be lenient.

Why does Paul make such a point of this? Not because Paul feels personally slighted or offended by the sins of the Corinthians. Not because Paul himself is not getting the respect due him. No. The honor of Christ is at stake (v. 3). Paul is Christ's apostle. To reject Paul's call to repentance is to reject Christ's call to repentance. Jesus said, "The one who hears you hears Me; and the one who rejects you rejects Me, and the one who rejects Me rejects Him who sent Me" (Luke 10:16).

Paul's opponents in Corinth were demanding proof that Christ was speaking through Paul. Christ had not been weak in dealing with them; He had been powerful among them. Paul has pointed to the signs, wonders, and miracles that had been done among them (12:12). Paul was Christ's representative, and Christ was speaking and acting through Paul. Christ's power had already been evident among the Corinthians in the miraculous signs Christ had done through Paul; now Christ's power would be evident also in words spoken through Paul.

Jesus appeared to be weak when He was crucified, yet Jesus lives by God's power (vv. 3b–4). He had made Himself nothing (Philippians 2:7). He had made Himself beggarly poor (8:9). His apparent weakness brought the taunts and jeers of those religious leaders who considered themselves powerful and important: "He saved others; He cannot save Himself! He's the King of Israel;

let Him come down now from the cross, and we will believe in Him. He trusts in God; let God deliver Him now, if He desires Him. For He said, 'I am the Son of God'" (Matthew 27:42–43).

Jesus was declared "to be the Son of God in power . . . by His resurrection from the dead" (Romans 1:4).

In the same way, Paul is weak in Christ (v. 4b). Paul shares the lot of his despised and scorned Savior in this world. Just as Jesus' opponents despised and scorned Him, Paul's opponents despise and scorn him. But by God's power Paul also lives with Christ to serve the Corinthians. Paul will show himself to be very much alive, united with Christ in His power and in doing Christ's work. Outwardly, to the eyes of the world, Paul may appear weak, but he proclaims the Gospel—the power of God for the salvation of all including the Corinthians.

Let's pause for a moment to consider how the principle Paul is expressing here is still true today. Think about this: The Word of God—whether preached, taught, read, or studied—appears weak, no different than the sentences and paragraphs on the pages of any other book. People have the power to tune out or disregard what is preached and taught and to refuse to consider what they have heard or read. Holy Baptism looks like only simple water. Its power can easily be dismissed. Holy Communion appears to consist of simple bread and wine—again, a mere custom that can easily be rejected or ignored.

Nevertheless, despite their evident weakness, the Word and Sacraments carry the power of God Himself. God's Word brings sinners to repentance. This Word brings life, eternal life, to all who believe it. This Word delivers us from the guilt of our sins and from eternal death. God has connected His powerful Word to the Sacraments. The Word and the Sacraments are the power (the "dynamite") of God for salvation. The Word cuts back and forth, exposing sin and healing the sinner. The Word has power because it is the Lord's Word, and He is powerful beyond our comprehension.

Paul may have appeared weak to the eyes of his unbelieving opponents, but he was actually plugged into the power of the Gospel. Christianity today may appear to be weak and ineffective to unbelievers, but we Christians are plugged into that same life-giving, healing power of the Gospel—the sword of the Spirit—that Paul wielded.

2 A Call for Self-Examination (13:5–10)

Despite the power of the Word, some in Corinth apparently demanded more proof that Christ spoke through Paul. So now Paul calls on the Corinthians to supply some proof of who *they* were. "Examine yourselves, to see whether you are in the faith. Test yourselves," he says (v. 5). Now it was *their* turn. Were *they* in the faith? Here the word *faith* refers to the *what* of the faith, its content. Were the Corinthians still holding to that which God's people believe, teach, and confess? *Had* the Gospel been preached to them by Paul? *Had* they come to confess the faith? If they pass that test, then Paul is vindicated. If Christ is in them, then they are in the faith—and Paul is a true apostle (v. 6), the one whose labor had by grace brought them to true faith.

If Christ controls their lives, then they *are* in the faith. In his Letter to the Galatians, Paul stated in memorable words what it means to be in Christ: "I have been crucified with Christ. It is no longer I who live, but Christ who lives in me. And the life I now live in the flesh, I live by faith in the Son of God, who loved me and gave Himself for me" (Galatians 2:20).

What was true of Paul would also be true of the Corinthians—unless they had failed to receive the Gospel. And if they had failed to receive the Gospel, then Paul had failed as an apostle of the Gospel. But Paul trusts that they will discover that he has *not* been a failure. If Paul's work among them has been marked with success, that will be evident in the faith that the Corinthians confess. That is the real purpose for their self-examination—to see that they *are* Christians; if they are, then Paul is a genuine apostle.

Today also the Gospel leaves its mark; when the Gospel is proclaimed purely, then it will create Christians. The Gospel creates the Church, and the presence of believing Christians shows that the Gospel is being proclaimed. Do we want assurance that God is at work among us and within us? Look for faith. The presence of faith in Christ within you and others is clear proof that God is at work through the Gospel.

So Paul prays for his beloved Corinthians (v. 7). He prays that they will not do what is wrong. God also is able to preserve Christians in the true faith; in fact, God alone is able to keep Christians from evil. As our Lord taught in the Lord's Prayer, so Paul prayed that the Corinthians would not be led into temptation, but that they would be delivered from evil. He does not want them to fail.

And, even though the Corinthians' faith vindicates Paul's apostleship, Paul's concern is not for his personal reputation. His prayer is not selfish. He is not asking God to preserve the Corinthians in faith so that people will think the better of him, so that it will be evident that *he* has not been a failure. Rather he asks God that the Corinthians will do what is right, *even if* Paul were to appear to have been a failure. For if they do what is right, there will be no need for Paul to take any action when he comes to Corinth.

As God's servant, Paul cannot do anything against the truth (v. 8); he can only work for the truth. Falsehood belongs to the evil one; he is a liar and the father of lies (John 8:44). The very nature of sin is that it turns the truth about God into a lie (Romans 1:25). Truth is found in Jesus; He *is* the Truth (John 14:6). As Christians, the Corinthians had been taught in accordance with the truth that is in Jesus (Ephesians 4:21). They knew that love does not delight in evil, but rejoices with the truth (1 Corinthians 13:6).

So Paul was glad whenever he was weak but they were strong (v. 9). In praying for them to be perfected, Paul was praying for their complete restoration. He prayed that they might become mature, attaining to the whole measure of the fullness of Christ (Ephesians 4:13). That's God's will for all His people—you and me, too. We know that process will never be complete in this life. Yet, despite all the difficulties and setbacks experienced by the Corinthians, Paul prays that the process may go forward and that their restoration will be complete in the day of Christ. And we can pray the same thing for ourselves and for one another.

In his letters, Paul has had to be harsh with the Corinthians; that had been difficult for him. He had not relished that task. He took no particular pleasure in laying down the Law. No minister of the Gospel does. Condemning and punishing people is not something God Himself enjoys; He takes no pleasure in condemning the wicked. And if God receives no enjoyment from condemning and punishing, then certainly God's servants cannot take pleasure in condemning sinners, either.

What God does enjoy is saving sinners from death, redeeming them for eternal life, and forgiving their sins. The same wonderful, saving work is also the supreme pleasure of God's servants. Sharing the Good News of God's grace through Christ is the real joy of Christians. So Paul writes as he does—harshly, calling upon the Corinthians to leave their sins and to repent—so that it will not be necessary for him to deal harshly, severely, or rigorously with them when he comes (v. 10a).

Paul would rather use his authority as an apostle to build the Corinthians up, not to tear them down. That edifying work is Paul's purpose as Christ's apostle. He had not been called to condemn the Corinthians for their sins, but to build them up in their faith in Christ. As Paul had written earlier (10:8), he *does* have authority to tear down, to wreck, the strongholds of those who are enemies of the cross of Christ (10:4–5). But the Corinthians are not Paul's enemies. They are his dear friends whom he loves. Paul longs to use his authority to build them up.

The same is true of the authority of pastors and spiritual leaders in the Church today. The authority of the pastoral office is not for the purpose of putting God's people down, but to build them up. Pastors—and the whole Church—have the happy task of announcing to sinners the grace of God. Pastors, as the servants of God who are called to proclaim the Gospel to the public, have the wonderful privilege—in the place and by the command of the Lord Jesus—to forgive sinners of all their sins.

3 A Call for Action (13:11–13)

Paul has come to the end. "Finally, brothers, rejoice"—which is more than "good-bye." Actually, the Greek word, which appears as "good-bye" in some translations at the end of a letter, is the same word that is most often translated "rejoice." Paul has, in fact, used this same word to mean "rejoice" twice in this letter (in 6:10 and 7:7). So there is more than a "good-bye" here. Paul leaves the Corinthians with an encouragement to rejoice. (And, by the way, the same Greek word was often also used as a "hello" at the beginning of letters—but not in this letter. At the beginning of 2 Corinthians, Paul used another "hello" word—the word that is translated "grace" (1:2). So, just as Paul began this letter with a "hello" that was more than a mere "hello," so he ends this letter with a "good-bye" that is more than a mere "good-bye.")

This "rejoice" is followed by four more encouragements. The first of these admonitions is "aim for perfection" or, literally, "be restored to restoration" (the same word is used in 13:9). Paul had written in order to restore the Corinthians to the proper condition; they are to let his words have their full effect. The second admonition is "comfort one another." The third admonition is "agree with one another" or, literally, "think in the same way." The fourth admonition is "live in peace." This encouragement echoes the command of Jesus, "be at peace with one another" (Mark 9:50).

"And the God of love and peace will be with you." Paul frequently makes use of this heartening reminder at the end of his letters. What an encouraging way to take leave, with the reminder that the God who gives us peace through Jesus is with us. We might well take an example from this way in which Paul customarily takes leave of his dear Christian friends, with the affirmation that the God who has brought us peace through our Savior will keep us in His peace until we next meet.

Where God's love and peace are at work, God's people live together in fellowship. Therefore, Paul urges the Corinthians to greet one another with a holy kiss. In the Middle East, the kiss was the sign of peace and love. The kiss was exchanged between men and men and between women and women. It was the outward sign of inner unity, the visible token that the community was truly reconciled in Christ (Matthew 5:23–24). It became a regular part of the church's liturgy. Only people who could exchange the peace of the Lord could receive His body and blood in the Lord's Supper. Those who were not reconciled could not come to the Table of the Lord. In the light of all of the problems that threatened to split the Corinthian congregation into warring camps, and that threatened to divide the entire congregation from Paul, its spiritual father, perhaps some might have wondered whether they could go on exchanging a kiss of peace. Paul assures them that it is proper (v. 12).

Then he reminds the Corinthians that not only are they still united in Christ with one another but with brothers and sisters in Christ everywhere. "All the saints greet you" (v. 13). In their struggles they were not alone. Their fellow believers, made holy by the same blood of Christ, by the same Baptism, by the outpouring of the same Holy Spirit, were in full partnership with them, "fellow citizens with the saints and members of the household of God" (Ephesians 2:19).

4 A Word of Blessing (13:14)

Paul concludes with words that have come to be known as the apostolic benediction. This blessing is no mere wish for something to happen; no "may" is needed here. This blessing actually bestows what the words name—the blessing of the Holy Trinity. God's servants who speak it put the name of God on His people, and, in doing so, bless them. The Lord Jesus Christ is the one who brings grace, God the Father is the one who brings love, the Holy Spirit is the one who brings fellowship. All are the gifts of the Holy Trinity to us.

Note too that the way the blessing is stated shows us the way we receive it: the grace of Christ leads us to the love of God, and the love of God when put into place in our lives through the Spirit produces fellowship with God and with other believers. The grace of the Lord Jesus Christ, and the love of God, and the fellowship of the Holy Spirit are with all of us. Of that we can be sure. We have God's Word and promise. To this we can only say, "Amen!"

A Postscript

What did this letter accomplish among the Corinthians? Did it have the desired results? Was Paul received in Corinth with joy or sorrow? Luke tells us that Paul traveled through Macedonia, "[giving] them much encouragement." He later spent three months in Greece (Acts 20:1–3). He had planned to sail from there to Syria, probably from the port of Cenchrea. Because of a plot against him from the Jews, he doubled back through Macedonia, accompanied by the men delegated to take the offering to Jerusalem (8:23).

During his stay at Corinth, Paul wrote to the church at Rome. His work in the East was done, and his mind was set on the West. Paul is satisfied with the way things have turned out: "At present, however, I am going to Jerusalem bringing aid to the saints. For Macedonia and Achaia have been pleased to make some contribution for the poor among the saints at Jerusalem. They were pleased to do it, and indeed they owe it to them. For if the Gentiles have come to share in their spiritual blessings, they ought also to be of service to them in material blessings. When therefore I have completed this and have delivered to them what has been collected, I will leave for Spain by way of you" (Romans 15:25–28). From everything we know, the Word of the Spirit through Paul had done its work.

And what does this letter say to us? We, the Church today, also sometimes contend with problems that threaten to divide and weaken us. We struggle with strained relationships. The devil is still at it. He still uses distortions of the Gospel to drive wedges between Christians.

But we have seen how God, working through Paul, reunited a divided and troubled congregation—restoring relationships between the members themselves and between the congregation and the apostle Paul, their spiritual leader. Paul dealt with the problems in Corinth directly, but also with grace and in love. He spoke the truth. He said what needed to be said. But he did it out of a heart full of love and concern.

Paul was not afraid to expose his own weaknesses and fears. He did not bulldoze over people, pulling rank indiscriminately. He did not overpower the Corinthians with the sheer force of his personality or by simply asserting the authority of his office and dismissing the concerns of those he led. He acted directly and persistently, but with evident love and with patience.

Yes, we can learn much from Paul as he worked as the Spirit's instrument to reknit his own relationship with a congregation that had become estranged from him and as he reknit also the unity within this fractured congregation. And we can pray that our Lord would continue to work the same unity among us that He worked among the believers in Corinth. That unity will not reach perfection while we live in the Church on earth. But we can grow in it. And we can look forward to the Last Day when perfect unity of the Spirit and of the faith will be ours, God's gift of grace, in the new heaven and the new earth.

Concluding Activities

End with a brief prayer, perhaps thanking God for His blessing upon this LifeLight course and asking the Lord to preserve us in our faith and Christian life and fellowship. You may also want to read the apostolic benediction together. Then make any necessary announcements (perhaps including information about the next LifeLight course).

Small-Group Leaders Material

God's Comfort in Affliction

2 Corinthians 1:1–11

Preparing for the Session

Central Focus

Paul found comfort in his afflictions from the God of all comfort, and Paul's own experience of this comfort overflowed into the comfort he passed along to the Christians of Corinth.

Objectives

That participants, led by the Holy Spirit, will

1. understand more fully the comfort we receive from God through the Gospel;
2. desire to share the comfort that overflows in our own lives as we are comforted by the God of all comfort; and
3. pass along to others in their sufferings the comfort with which we have been comforted by God.

For the Small-Group Leader

Small-Group Discussion Helps

Day 1 • 2 Corinthians 1:1

1. The first question provides a quick review of the contents of 1 Corinthians. If some group members did not participate in the LifeLight course on 1 Corinthians, you may want to spend more time in review for their sake, without, of course, making the time tedious for the others. Problems in the church at Corinth at the time of Paul's first letter included divisions and a lack of spiritual unity among the members of the Corinthian congregation; sexual immorality of the worst kind that had gone unaddressed; ungodly lawsuits and public bickering; some believers were continuing the pagan practice of engaging in sexual immorality with temple prostitutes associated with the worship of the goddess Diana; disagreements concerning whether or not to eat food that had been sacrificed to idols; the Lord's Supper was being desecrated by a lack of concern for and unity among the communicants; and, finally, some of the Corinthian Christians did not believe in the resurrection of the dead.

2. This question may cause some participants to want to rehearse congregational disagreements they've experienced or to criticize the handling of such problems. Avoid this by asking the group to focus on answering the question itself. When confronted by disagreements in a congregation, some people become very disillusioned. If this appears to have happened to some in your group, remind them that every congregation is made up of people and pastors who are both sinners and saints at the same time. Two ways of dealing with these problems might be suggested. One is to pray for the people involved. A second is to address the problem forthrightly and kindly. In other words, attack the issue, not the people involved. Or, as Henry Ford once put it, "Don't find fault, find a solution."

3. (a) Timothy was from Lystra, situated in modern-day Turkey. His mother was Jewish and his father Greek. Upon the solid recommendation of fellow Christians in the churches of the area, Paul took Timothy along on his journeys. Paul circumcised Timothy, probably to remove a potential obstacle to his ministry among Jews. (b) Timothy had been influenced by the spirituality of his mother Eunice and his grandmother Lois. (c) These women had exposed Timothy to the Scriptures from his earliest years. (d) Paul had directed Timothy, apparently a young pastor/evangelist among the believers by then, to remain in Ephesus to address some problems in that church.

Day 2 • 2 Corinthians 1:2–3

4. Paul uses greetings like the one in verse 2 repeatedly. (a) In view of the many problems of the Corinthians and the scolding that Paul had administered to them in 1 Corinthians, they were undoubtedly yearning for the grace of God—the free, unearned, undeserved gift of God's mercy and forgiveness revealed in Jesus Christ. (b) Peace is the balm of God's love that soothes our pain and takes away our guilt. It assures us that God has accepted, approved, and adopted us in Christ.

5. This question gives participants a chance to share a personal experience. It is possible that some of the group members will not feel comfortable with this. Respect that. You may be able to break the ice by being

prepared briefly to provide an example from your own experience. Invite only volunteers to share their own examples; don't force anyone to do so.

6. (a) The Lord saw the circumstances of the enslaved children of Israel and had compassion on them, appointing Moses to be His spokesman. (b) God had compassion on the repentant inhabitants of Nineveh. (c) Jesus saw the harassed and helpless people and had compassion on them. In all three cases, we see the Lord's concern for people—for the distress of their daily lives and for their spiritual distress when they live without Him. In each case, His compassion led Him not just to *feel* compassion for them, but to come to help them.

7. (a) These famous words of comfort are meant to soothe the suffering of Israel. They convey the Lord's abundant mercy and the forgiveness of sins. Their context is that period when the Jews were held in a seventy-year-long exile in Babylon. (b) Jesus saw the confusion and sadness of His disciples and comforted them by pointing them to their home in heaven. (c) With a single word, Jesus brought overwhelming comfort to the despairing and weeping Mary Magdalene on the morning of His resurrection.

Day 3 • 2 Corinthians 1:4

8. Paul does not tell us how God comforts people. He simply states that He does. Participants may point to any of the several ways God's Word comes to us: the hearing and reading of a sermon or the Bible, time spent in public worship, reading a devotional book, or receiving the caring ministry of a pastor or a friend. (Note that in Psalm 119 "the Law" refers to the entirety of God's written Word.)

9. God's comfort is meant to be enjoyed by experiencing it first ourselves and then sharing it with others.

10. This question asks for personal sharing; accept responses from volunteers. As participants talk about point b, most will probably acknowledge that sharing God's comfort with someone going through a trial similar to one we ourselves have experienced often brings back some of the pain of that trial, but God's comfort also comes flooding back in all its fullness too.

Day 4 • 2 Corinthians 1:4–5

11. God's Spirit has been at work in His suffering people. His Word of grace has often made them more sensitive to and compassionate toward those who are suffering.

12. The unique comfort we bring is the Lord's mercy, His love, and His promises of hope and help. We receive this comfort from the Gospel, which comes to us in the Word and in the Sacraments.

13. (a) Let participants offer suggestions. The media sometimes ridicules the Christian faith. Some believers suffer ridicule on the job for their beliefs or ethics. (b) Jesus says those who are persecuted "for righteousness' sake" are blessed—accepted and approved by God. He works in us the ability to "let our light shine" in this sin-darkened world and then He gives the strength to stand up under persecution that results from our witness.

Day 5 • 2 Corinthians 1:5–11

14. In his sufferings Paul experienced the overflowing, super-abundance of Christ's comfort. (Although Paul speaks in the plural, the context indicates that Paul is referring to himself. This use of the plural is sometimes referred to as the editorial plural.)

15. Paul thought of the Corinthians as he suffered. He rejoiced that his suffering would benefit them and others because he was persecuted in the first place for bringing the Gospel to people. Apparently the Corinthians were themselves also experiencing suffering for the faith. Paul was comforted because he knew that the same comfort of God that overflowed for him when he suffered would overflow in the lives of the Corinthians.

16. So intense was the persecution that Paul despaired of his life. But the result of his suffering and stress was that he learned to rely entirely on God, not on himself.

17. The Lord delivered Paul from his peril as a result of the intercession of God's people. Paul placed great importance on intercessory prayer.

18. As we pray for others who are suffering—and encourage them by letting them know of our prayers on their behalf—we and they will praise and thank God together as He answers these prayers of intercession.

The Ministry of Divine Triumph

2 Corinthians 1:12–2:17

Preparing for the Session

Central Focus

Despite anxieties and pain as we serve Christ, we nevertheless participate in the divine triumph of the Gospel.

Objectives

That participants, led by the Holy Spirit, will

1. know that participation in the Church's Gospel ministry will involve pain as well as joy;
2. become more patient and trustful as God works through the Gospel; and
3. thank God for the wonderful privilege of having a place in the triumphant procession of the Gospel.

For the Small-Group Leader

Small-Group Discussion Helps

Day 1 • 2 Corinthians 1:12–19

1. (a) Paul "boasts" that "we behaved in the world with simplicity and godly sincerity, not by earthly wisdom but by the grace of God, and supremely so toward you." From the outset, Paul contrasts himself with his detractors and with those false teachers who had poisoned the air by accusing Paul of being a faithless, inept, insincere preacher. While they boasted of their superiority, Paul made his boast in Christ. (b) "Simplicity" and "godly sincerity" sometimes impress a few people in the world, but more often the world thinks of these qualities as quite unimpressive. Power, glitz, or wealth tend to impress them more. As we will see later, Paul's detractors expressed disappointment that Paul wasn't a more dynamic speaker, that he did not resort to more intellectually impressive arguments or to a more pleasing methodology when he presented the Gospel.

2. (a) "Simplicity" refers to a life set apart for God and His service, a life that, in thankfulness to God, is free of the kind of habitual, outward sins that would detract from the Gospel. Paul did not mean that he was without sin, for no one, obviously, can make that claim. By God's grace, however, he was growing in faith and in obedience to Christ. God clearly intends that the Christian is to be a faithful example to others of what the new life in the Spirit looks like. This is especially required of pastors and other church leaders. (b) The key words that signal to us that the "simplicity and godly sincerity" of which Paul writes do not simply indicate a holier-than-thou attitude are *from God* and *according to God's grace.* Neither holiness nor sincerity are possible without the power of God.

3. Paul was earnestly intent on communicating clearly with the Corinthians. As they clearly understood him, they would be able to share fully in the benefits of the Gospel with Paul and would be able to stand with Paul on Judgment Day in the righteousness of Jesus, their Savior.

4. Paul's plans called for him to visit the Corinthians both on his way to and on his way from Macedonia so they and he would be benefited twice by his visitation. However, Paul was for some reason unable to visit them at this time; or, perhaps due to the problems there and their need to work through these problems by themselves, he was unwilling to visit them at this point. It is possible that he visited them on his way from Macedonia but not on his way to there.

5. Paul's detractors used his change of plans as an opportunity to question his sincerity, integrity, and honesty, quite probably accusing him of saying one thing and doing another. These detractors may have contrasted themselves with Paul, assuring the Corinthians that they themselves were too spiritual for such dishonesty! A convincing argument can often be made about someone's motives or character when that person is not present to answer.

6. (a) God sent His Son Jesus to save us, not to condemn us! (b) Even though we were sinners, Christ died for us; that is how much God loves us! (c) Jesus promises eternal life to those who believe and trust in Him; He assures us that no one—not even the devil himself—can thwart God's determination to save us. Encourage participants to express these Gospel affirmations in personal terms.

Day 2 • 2 Corinthians 1:20–22

7. (a) In Jesus, we can be confident that God will keep each and every one of the promises He has made to us. As Romans 8:32 clearly says, since God held back nothing—not even His own Son—to secure our salvation, we can be sure that He will withhold no other good thing. (b) This question is marked for personal reflection. Let volunteers share both their personal experiences with God's faithfulness to His Word of promise and their response of worship to that faithfulness.

8. Let participants comment. The verses assure us that we need not rely on our own strength. God is the one who makes it possible for us to stand firm in Christ. Three phrases in the passage refer us back to our Baptism. There we were "anointed" with the Holy Spirit, just as Christ was in His Baptism. There we received God's "seal," and there the Holy Spirit came to indwell us. This Spirit is God's "guarantee" that He will finish the work He began in us. Someone concerned about his or her own strength of faith needs to focus instead on the faithfulness of God who began this good work in us and who will bring it to completion in the Day of Jesus Christ (Philippians 1:6).

Day 3 • 2 Corinthians 1:23–2:4

9. Various answers may be given by participants. Ordinarily, we avoid someone when we have had a disagreement with them and something hurtful has been said or done. At that point, feelings may be too tense, things may be said that we or others may regret. Both we and the other person may need a cooling-off period. We hope that all involved will be ready at a later and better time to talk things out and find reconciliation. But the danger in this approach lies in the fact that the matter may never be addressed, and a grudge could develop. Hardened attitudes in one or both parties to the dispute could forever stand in the way of reconciliation. Some problems need to be addressed and resolved face-to-face right away; time will only magnify them and make resolution more difficult. We need God's divine wisdom to know when to do what, and His courage to follow that divine wisdom even when our sinful nature would choose to do just the opposite. In times of conflict, we need to ask our Lord for both! Without Him, sin and Satan will pollute and ruin relationships over and over again in our lives.

10. (a) Paul wanted to avoid lording it over the Corinthians—that is, dealing with them with an attitude of superiority and harshness. Rather, he was aiming at their being led by the Spirit to resolve their problems and thereby once again discover Christian joy. (b) When those in leadership are tempted to lord it over the flock of Jesus Christ, they can develop an attitude of spiritual superiority that is just the opposite of the humility Christ Himself both demonstrates Himself and commands in His under-shepherds. This can lead them to "drive" the flock in harshness rather than to lead it in gentleness. The sinful nature being what it is will cause some sheep to simply wander away and be lost and other sheep to rebel and possibly even attack the shepherd. Either way, the individual members of the congregation and the pastor, too, will lose their focus on Christ's mission. Do not allow anyone in the group to "confess" someone else's sins. Rather, encourage one another to pray for your shepherd(s) and for yourselves, asking God to give both congregation leaders and members gentle, teachable spirits and humble, Christlike concern for one another.

11. Paul truly expected that by God's power the Corinthians would work out their problems and deficiencies. Even before this had happened, Paul had begun to anticipate the joy they would experience when it did. His confidence would have led them, too, to be confident that the Lord would work in and through them.

12. Verse 4 indicates that Paul's words were motivated by sincere grief and concern for them as their spiritual father (see 1 Corinthians 4:15). If he had not cared so much about them, he would not have bothered to bring their sins to their attention. This would have proven a much smoother, easier route. The fact that he did take them severely to task—while interpreted by some as a lack of concern for their feelings—showed that he truly cared about them. Apathy toward sin is far worse than anger toward sin!

13. Encourage participants to share their own experiences; such experiences are common enough that almost everyone has had one—either on the giving or receiving end.

Day 4 • 2 Corinthians 2:5–11

14. A member of the Corinthian congregation was having sexual relations with his father's wife (most likely not his mother, but his stepmother).

15. Paul urged the Corinthians to put the offender out

of the church so that he would see the seriousness of his sin and the spiritual danger to which he had left himself vulnerable. Such open unrepentant sin expressed the reality of his loss of faith.

16. (a) The Corinthians had carried out Paul's suggestion. But they had gone farther. Even when the offender repented and grieved for his sin, the congregation continued to shun him. Paul states that the punishment was sufficient; it was severe and had gone on long enough. If they did not now express complete forgiveness toward this repentant man, he could be overwhelmed by excessive sorrow, and thus be lost forever. (b) So Paul asks the Corinthians to forgive the repentant sinner and give him their love once again. He especially needed restoration to the Christian fellowship as a brother in Christ and acceptance as a sinner whom God had completely forgiven. (c) Paul offered his own forgiveness and the assurance of Christ's forgiveness.

17. **Challenge Question.** This is marked as a challenge question because some may find the two word pictures used by the prophet Isaiah difficult. The verse is written in poetic form. The first image tells us that God does not wish to "break" repentant sinners; the second word picture says that He does not want to "quench" such a person's faith. Rather, in mercy and grace, our Lord wants to encourage and strengthen that faith. What wonderful comfort this passage speaks to all of us repentant sinners!

Day 5 • 2 Corinthians 2:12–17

18. Paul saw the Lord opening doors for him in his ministry. The door that was opened was a willingness on the part of the people of Troas to listen to Paul and his Gospel message.

19. Encourage participants to share instances from their own experiences in which they saw God guiding and leading them in specific directions, especially as they served others in the name of Christ.

20. Paul expressed his thankfulness for the opportunities God gave him to proclaim the Gospel and so to have a part in the coming of God's gracious kingdom into this world. Sinners were being forgiven and brought into the Lord's kingdom. Despite what appeared to be setbacks, the Gospel of salvation was being proclaimed, and the Holy Spirit was leading people to faith. Paul saw this as the Lord's "triumphal procession."

21. **Challenge Question.** Paul extends the image of the incense used in Roman processions to another spiritual truth. To believers the "incense" of the Gospel is so sweet! It is the fragrance of life! But to those who meet the Gospel with unbelief and hostility, their rejection means eternal death in hell. Because their reaction to the Gospel seals their judgment to condemnation, the "incense" of the Gospel is the smell of death.

22. Many among the false teachers apparently charged fees for their services, giving the impression that God's grace was for sale. Paul, in contrast, was motivated by his calling from God to share the Gospel freely.

23. Encourage participants to share insights, and as time will allow, individual prayer requests with one another.

Great Treasure in Earthen Vessels

2 Corinthians 3:1–5:10

Preparing for the Session

Central Focus

Though we have the ministry of the new covenant, which far exceeds the glory of the old covenant, we bear this treasure in the clay jars of our earthly existence. Even so, by God's grace, the glory of Christ shines through us to others.

Objectives

That participants, led by the Holy Spirit, will develop

1. a keener awareness of the surpassing glory of the Gospel;
2. a greater appreciation for the treasure of the Gospel even though it comes to us in the weak vessels of this earthly life; and
3. a greater sense of confidence and steadfastness in remaining faithful to the Gospel despite the hardships to which we are subject in this life.

For the Small-Group Leader

Small-Group Discussion Helps

Day 1 • 2 Corinthians 3:1–6

1. Throughout this letter we read comments that reveal Paul's continuing concern about the false teachers who were distorting his ministry and doing great harm to the cause of the Gospel in Corinth. In order to infiltrate the Corinthian congregation, the false teachers had managed to deceive the believers. They did this in two ways: by boasting about themselves and their superior teachings while condemning Paul and by presenting letters of recommendation from prominent church leaders—letters that were undoubtedly forgeries.

2. Paul was able to point to the Corinthian Christians themselves and claim them as his living letters of recommendation. Paul had been among them and served them freely with the Gospel, and he knew that they knew it. Group participants may be able to point to the influence of Christian parents, relatives, pastors, Sunday School teachers, friends, or other Bible students who helped them come to faith or grow in faith. Others "read" of this influence as they see the new life in Christ that the participants live daily.

3. **Challenge Question.** The "tablets of stone" in verse 3 call to mind the two tablets of stone on which the Lord wrote the Ten Commandments. Moses carried them from Mount Sinai to the people of Israel. "Tablets of human hearts" refers to the new heart that God the Holy Spirit produces in us when we come to faith. Contrasted with stone, as the references in Jeremiah and Ezekiel point out, the "heart tablet" has been softened by the love of Christ. In this terminology, Paul graphically contrasts the old and the new covenants.

4. In verses 4–5, Paul asserts that, unlike the false teachers who want to claim the credit, everything he has done has been instigated and empowered by God—from his first coming to faith to his sharing the Good News with them.

5. (a) The Law kills by insisting that we keep the Law of God perfectly in every point. (b) It's impossible to do this, so the Law puts us under God's curse when we try to stand before God based on our performance. Only by faith may we stand. (c) The Law kills because the sinful nature cannot keep its requirements; the Law can only condemn the sin it finds in us. The Gospel comforts us with the assurance that Christ has fulfilled the requirements of the Law in our place, He died to secure forgiveness for all our sins, and now He enables us to obey God's Law through the Spirit who lives within our hearts.

Day 2 • 2 Corinthians 3:7–18

6. Moses' face became radiant because he had been in the presence of God; it reflected God's glory.

7. Paul refers to the old covenant as a ministry of death because that's precisely what it brought when we failed to live up to its requirements; even so, it came from God and thus came with His glory.

8. (a) The ministry of the Law only condemns, while the ministry of the Gospel brings righteousness (Christ's own right standing with God) through the for-

giveness of sins. (b) Furthermore, the glory that came with the old covenant is fading, but the glory that comes with the new covenant lasts eternally.

9. Verse 17 refers especially to a freedom from the Law and its demands as a way of pleasing God. Since these demands have been met for us by Christ, our Substitute, they no longer enslave us. We are free. Paul says much the same thing in Romans 8:1–2, where he asserts that we have been set free from the power of sin and death.

10. As time will allow, let volunteers pray their prayers aloud, or save these and use them as you close your time of small-group discussion.

Day 3 • 2 Corinthians 4:1–6

11. We might well lose heart if we had only our own resources on which to rely. But we can find comfort in God's power and furthermore in His mercy and grace. He forgives our sins and shortcomings. His love for us is so much greater than any love we might imagine. Remembering all these things—and more—about our wonderful God will surely keep us, too, from losing heart in the face of frustrations and opposition.

12. (a) Satan uses intellectualism, materialism, secularism, sexuality, power, and many other schemes to keep spiritually blind people from seeing the truth and to induce spiritual blindness in those who believe. (b) Only by the power of the Holy Spirit can spiritual sight be created in those blinded by Satan. Our Lord chooses to use our witness, but He must produce the results in the hearts and minds of those to whom we speak. Accordingly, prayer plays a critical role in evangelistic outreach.

13. The bottom line for Paul is preaching Christ crucified and serving Christ's people.

14. When the light of faith shines in our hearts, we are able to discern, to know God's glory as it has been revealed in Christ. In other words, faith looks to Christ. Seeing Christ, we also see the Father and His gracious love for us. Together we live in fellowship in God's love.

Day 4 • 2 Corinthians 4:7–18

15. In the term *jars of clay,* Paul refers to himself and his fellow ministers. Paul is saying that, in and of himself, he is weak and expendable. However, he has the privilege of serving as a vessel who contains and conveys the treasure of the Gospel. Paul rejoices in being an ordinary human being because it means that no one could mistake him for the treasure or his power for the power of God.

16. Paul was *afflicted* but *not crushed; perplexed* but *not driven to despair; persecuted* but *not forsaken; struck down* but *not destroyed.* (Various translations will use different terms that express the same thoughts.) Encourage participants to recount experiences in which they felt these same ways.

17. Paul's ultimate goal is that both he and the Corinthian believers be received by God in the presence of Christ in heaven.

18. Our outer nature is *wasting away*; our inner nature is *being renewed.* Our *slight momentary affliction* is achieving an *eternal weight of glory.* What is seen is *transient.* What is unseen is *eternal.* Such an outlook results from a confidence that comes from faith in God, who loves us in Christ.

19. Encourage participants to describe experiences that might have caused them to lose heart but through which God sustained them with His power and love.

Day 5 • 2 Corinthians 5:1–10

20. Many things in our fallen, sinful world cause us to groan: sickness, cruelty, hatred, war and bloodshed, crime, injustice, death, unbelief, apathy, loneliness, insensitivity . . . the list could go on and on.

21. God has made us ultimately for the purpose of living with Him forever in eternity.

22. Paul prefers to be in heaven. Yet, since we have no power over this, and since we belong to the Lord whether on earth or in heaven, our goal is to please God.

The Ministry of Reconciliation

2 Corinthians 5:11–6:10

Preparing for the Session

Central Focus

A wonderful change has come about in our relationship with God since Christ has reconciled us to God. As the Lord's ambassadors and fellow workers with Christ, we implore others to be reconciled to God through faith in Christ.

Objectives

That participants, led by the Holy Spirit, will

1. know more deeply the fear and love of God that convinces us that Christ died for all and compels us to share the Gospel with others;
2. appreciate the privilege Christ has given us in making the Gospel known; and
3. show great endurance in commending the Gospel to others.

For the Small-Group Leader

Small-Group Discussion Helps

Day 1 • 2 Corinthians 5:11–15

1. The "fear of the Lord" (reverence and deep respect for God) motivated Paul. He knew that on Judgment Day he would appear before the Lord to give an account of his ministry. The Day of Judgment inspires awe, but not terror, in the hearts of believers. We know that Christ has taken away our sins and guilt, and thus also our terror at the thought of God's judgment.

2. The Corinthians surely knew Paul's sincerity of heart. They knew he was not trying to trick them so that he could somehow profit in a selfish or unethical way through his ministry. Paul wanted them to see the contrast between his ministry and that of his opponents, which was self-seeking and motivated by the hope for personal gain. Seeing this, they would be able to take pride in what God had accomplished in their midst through Paul and his sincere ministry of the Gospel.

3. (a) Paul's opponents also were claiming that Paul was insane—that he was a religious fanatic who had gone too far. (b) In reply, Paul asserted his complete devotion to the Lord and to those he served in the Lord's name. The unbelieving world, which understands neither faith nor faithfulness, may judge this to be insanity. Nevertheless, Paul's ministry was marked by his faithful teaching, the integrity of his life, and his love for his fellow believers. Recalling these characteristics, the believers at Corinth would surely attest to Paul's sanity.

4. Christ's love compelled Paul to preach the Gospel, no matter what the obstacles.

5. Verse 15 beautifully summarizes the life of the Christian. Because of all that Christ has done for us, especially through His death on the cross, we no longer have to live just for ourselves. Now we live for Jesus Christ. This life is a thankful, happy, delighted one!

Day 2 • 2 Corinthians 5:16–17

6. (a) If we view people from a worldly viewpoint, we will base our assessment of their worth on outward characteristics like their achievements, education, possessions, power, money, popularity, position in society, looks, personality, or whether they agree with us or think like we do or look like we do. (b) When we remember that Christ died for all and that Christians are a new creation of God, we can see others through the lens of the Gospel—with the attitude and mind of Christ. This changes our attitude toward both believers and unbelievers and therefore changes how we treat them.

7. (a) Looking at the way Paul persecuted Christ's followers, we can deduce that before his conversion Paul viewed Christ as merely a man, a troublemaker who had misled His followers. Evidently, the preconversion Paul believed that Jesus got what He deserved, because Paul set out to execute Jesus' followers too. It's also evident that before his conversion Paul rejected Christ's resurrection from the dead; if he had believed it, he would surely have acted differently toward Christ's followers. (b) The unbelieving world today holds many opinions of Christ. Some see Him as a prophet whose

teachings are wise, but hard to understand and harder to follow. Some see Him as a law-giver who demanded impossible things or as a mystical figure to whom we can pray for good luck or help when all else fails. Others view Jesus as a charlatan, or as a weak-kneed do-gooder, or as a historical figure we can safely ignore. Accept reasonable responses participants suggest.

8. When someone is "in Christ" that person has a living relationship with Jesus Christ as his or her Lord and Savior.

9. The "new creation" is nothing less than the recreated image of God which human beings lost when Adam and Eve fell into sin. It has to do with righteousness and purity, holiness and sinlessness. As the Holy Spirit works in us through His Word, God's people become "like Him" (1 John 3:2). His power makes this possible. In one sense, we are this "new creation" now. God has conferred on us the righteousness of Christ. In another sense, this "new creation" is a process. God continues to transform us into the image of His Son as He works in us through His means of grace.

10. (a) The "old" is our old Adam or old man, our sinful nature that is corrupt, dead, blind, and an enemy of God. (b) The new creation appears when we come into a living relationship with God through Jesus Christ. In Baptism, we died with Christ on His cross. Because this is true, sin's hold on us has been broken. Christ's life, His resurrected new life, now enables us to live as children of God. Scripture makes it clear that the old nature will continue to cling to us as long as we live here on earth. But Scripture makes it equally clear that our old nature can no longer make us sin or force us to rebel against God. Each day we can "drown" this old nature as we remember in repentance and faith Christ's cross and our Baptism. As God works in us through the power of the Gospel throughout our lives, we become ever more Christlike.

Day 3 • 2 Corinthians 5:18–21

11. Throughout his letters, Paul emphasizes the helplessness of sinners to save themselves and their desperate need for rescue, which is accomplished through Christ. The Bible describes us by nature as (a) spiritually blind, (b) spiritually dead, and (c) hostile toward God (or enemies of God).

12. (a) We are helpless to save ourselves. (b) Yet, in the midst of our sinfulness and powerlessness, Christ sacrificed Himself to save us.

13. (a) The Lord took our sins from us and placed them on Christ. Every sin that we have committed has been placed on Christ and was paid for by His death on the cross. In exchange, we received Christ's own righteousness. What a great exchange! (b) Just think of it! We have become righteous in God's sight. Let participants comment on ways this truth gives us hope for life here on earth and for life after our life on this earth ends.

14. An ambassador does not represent himself. An ambassador does not act on his personal authority and power. Ambassadors represent those who send them. As Christ's ambassador, Paul spoke on behalf of Christ. He delivered His message—His command and gracious invitation that people turn to Him for forgiveness and righteousness.

Day 4 • 2 Corinthians 6:1–2

15. The words of 2 Corinthians 6:1 amplify the plea in 2 Corinthians 5:20. In both verses, Paul implores the Corinthians to be reconciled to God. It would seem that some of the Corinthians, including quite possibly Paul's detractors, had heard, but not believed, the Gospel. Perhaps some had believed, but had placed themselves in danger of falling away. Thus, God's Word would be for them, not their salvation, but their judgment and damnation. It is difficult to know precisely what had caused the doubt and unbelief, but perhaps their doubting of Paul's authority had led them also to doubt the authority of the Gospel he preached.

16. (a) Various things can cause people to waste God's grace. When we continue in deliberate sin, we become blinded by sin, and our hearts become calloused to God's Word. This kind of sin might not involve external actions at all. We might live with an unforgiving heart toward someone who has wronged us. We might neglect God's Word or the Sacrament. We might listen to the Word every Sunday in church or read the Scriptures every day in our personal devotions, but not believe it or let it change our lives. Let participants mention other possibilities. (b) The Scriptures make it clear that we cannot keep ourselves in faith; God keeps us there. So we need to keep in contact with the Spirit's power through reading and hearing the Word, receiving the Lord's Supper, and remaining in fellowship with the community of believers.

17. Paul emphasizes the *now* because we may not have a *later*. When we are not right with God, we are wasting

opportunities to live for His praise and glory and in the joy of His sustaining presence.

18. Lists will vary, but may include activities like witnessing to others, forgiving someone a wrong, confronting someone about a sin, taking on a task at church where our time and talents could be used, charitable giving toward mission work, and such.

Day 5 • 2 Corinthians 6:3–10

19. Do not insist that participants answer this question aloud; instead, simply state that various things can get in the way of the Gospel when they distract us from God's grace or mislead us into trusting in things other than the Lord. Emphasize that God forgives our sins and shortcomings and helps us to overcome such roadblocks.

20. Paul endured beatings, imprisonments, riots, hard work, sleepless nights, and hunger. Allow participants to share specific ways their own hardships have presented witnessing opportunities.

21. Paul could and did also point to positive aspects of his ministry. These included times of glory and of good report; the acknowledgement by some of his genuine character; his position as an apostle; the opportunity to live in the power of Christ, to rejoice, and to make many rich with the treasures of the Gospel. Encourage participants to share some of the joys they experience in their own Christian lives.

22. (a) Paul comments that he has been dishonored, regarded as an imposter, and ignored. He does not tell us this all affected him, but doubtless such attacks would bring with them the temptation to discouragement. Paul may have been saddened by the attacks. Accept other reasonable responses. (b) Encourage participants to express ways such treatment in their own lives has affected them. Especially draw out any opportunities such attacks have provided to make a positive Gospel witness and to demonstrate Christian forgiveness and love.

23. (a) The Lord gave Paul many spiritual resources—purity, understanding, patience, kindness, sincere love, and truthful speech. (b) Encourage participants to comment on the resources God has made available to them to use in serving Him.

A Plea for Understanding

2 Corinthians 6:11–7:16

Preparing for the Session

Central Focus

Paul pleads with the Corinthians to open their hearts to him as he has opened his heart to them. The division between him and them is resolved by their repentance. Life in the Church today requires the same kind of openness and the same lifestyle of repentance for which Paul yearned and prayed in the Corinthian congregation.

Objectives

That participants, led by the Holy Spirit, will

1. know that a right relationship with fellow Christians results from a right relationship with God;
2. value Gospel-based Christian fellowship;
3. maintain a living relationship with God through His gifts of repentance and faith; and
4. maintain fellowship with other Christians through mutual forgiveness, love, and understanding.

For the Small-Group Leader

Small-Group Discussion Helps

Day 1 • 2 Corinthians 6:11–13

1. Paul has opened himself up to the Corinthians in verses 3–10, sharing with them not only the physical trials he has had to endure but also the emotional ones. With great intensity of feeling, Paul has allowed the Corinthians to see into his very heart. He has done this out of love for them. Thus, his heart is "wide open."

2. (a) People are normally willing to open themselves up to others and to speak freely when they share a relationship of mutual trust and respect. (b) If mutual trust and respect are missing, then people are usually unwilling to open themselves up to others. Often this happens because of past betrayals or other kinds of hurts.

3. Paul states in verse 12 that the Corinthians were holding back on their affection for him, even though he had expressed his affection and love for them. It is very possible that they did this because of the doubts about Paul that his detractors had planted in their minds. Also, at this point the Corinthians appear to have still been worldly and spiritually immature.

4. Paul longed for the Corinthians to open their hearts wide to him, just as he had opened his heart to them. He wanted the closeness, acceptance, and fellowship that mutual trust in a relationship brings. But Paul wasn't concerned about mere friendship. He was concerned about their acceptance and openness to the truth of the Gospel he had brought to them and that he wanted to continue to bring to them—both himself and through others.

5. This question is for personal reflection only. Accept comments from volunteers and share your own observations as you feel comfortable doing so. Every person can think of times when he or she has taken a risk only to be betrayed. In most cases, this makes us very reluctant to share anything with anyone that we don't know extremely well. We simply don't let others get to know us on any other than a surface level. As a result, we live lonelier and more isolated lives than we need to live. On the other hand, when we are able to be open to others, we find many benefits accruing from the relationships we develop. Openness permits us to enjoy genuine closeness, a feeling of connectedness with others, and a sense of unity that is not possible without openness.

6. In incredibly direct and beautiful words, Philippians 2:1–11 insists that we can be like Christ who willingly made Himself vulnerable, even to the point of allowing Himself to be crucified. The power to be vulnerable and the willingness to entrust ourselves to others is not foolhardy faith in other people, but complete trust in Christ. His servant posture is the one we can assume. For our trust is not placed in people but in Him, and thus we are not vulnerable in any truly important way. Christians share the same faith, the same Lord, the same need for forgiveness, and the same assurance of forgiveness and cleansing through Jesus Christ. As a result, they have a spiritual oneness that links them together. The reality of sin in others and our experience with the power of our old nature may cause even Christians to be hesitant

about sharing much about themselves with other Christians, at least at first. Trust builds over time. Remember, Paul had spent three years in Corinth. The apostle is not calling here for immediate and blind trust in anyone who claims to be a brother or sister in Christ. He is, however, addressing the refusal to work toward having the kind of vulnerable relationships Paul urged the Corinthians to have. As time will allow, ask the group to contrast the Philippians passage with John 2:24–25.

Day 2 • 2 Corinthians 6:14–7:1

7. (a) The opposites are righteousness and wickedness, light and darkness, Christ and Belial, believer and unbeliever, and the temple of God and idols. (b) Paul contrasts five total opposites, none of which bespeak a chance for compromise. Either spiritual life or spiritual death—that's the clear choice Paul presents.

8. Paul is implying that they could be led into wickedness, darkness, and the power of the devil and ultimately become unbelieving idolaters. In the struggle between Paul and his adversaries, the very Gospel of salvation and the immortal souls of the Corinthians were at stake.

9. Encourage participants to express the necessity that Christians today also separate themselves from the wickedness and evil that pervades so much of our own society. Examples might include sexual immorality, pornography and sexually-oriented entertainment, dishonest business practices, gambling, and other behaviors. Even when we cannot physically separate ourselves from such influences, we cannot support or participate in such evil. We can, however, attempt to influence others to avoid it, making plain the fact that such things do not please God.

10. Despite the seriousness of the situation, Paul still refers to the Corinthian believers as God's temple. He tells them that by virtue of this fact they must separate themselves from the false teachers.

11. (a) Let several volunteers share their paraphrases. In verse 18, God declares Himself to be the Father of believers and promises to claim them as His sons and daughters. (b) Again, let volunteers share. If no one mentions it, point out that in these verses we find encouragement to separate ourselves and purify ourselves from the wickedness of the unbelieving world around us, knowing that we are God's sons and daughters whose bodies and spirits are holy, dedicated to the Lord. Remembering who we are, we receive power from our Lord, and His Gospel promises to do what He asks of us.

Day 3 • 2 Corinthians 7:2–7

12. In verse 2, Paul maintains that he has treated the Corinthians fairly: He has wronged no one; he has corrupted no one; he has exploited no one. In verse 3, Paul affirms his loyalty to them: he would live or die with them. In verse 4, he declares his feelings toward them: he has great confidence in them and takes great pride in them. Ask participants which of these would draw the greatest response from them.

13. 2 Corinthians 2:12–13 and 7:5–7 indicate that Paul had found a receptive field among the people in Troas and had planned to remain there for a time to share the Gospel. However, when Titus did not come as expected, Paul became concerned and decided to go to Macedonia in order to join Titus. In Macedonia, Paul experienced extreme opposition, conflict, and fear. Titus finally appeared and brought Paul great comfort.

14. The message of comfort and encouragement that Paul received from Titus was his report that the Corinthians longed to see Paul, that they exhibited deep sorrow over their disobedience, and that they had expressed great concern for Paul's welfare. As a result of this favorable report, Paul says that his joy was greater than ever.

Day 4 • 2 Corinthians 7:8–12

15. Paul regretted for a time that the Corinthians were hurt by the letter he sent them. But, later, he was not sorry since the letter had brought the Corinthians to a godly sorrow that led them to repentance.

16. (a) Jesus instructs us to talk with other believers who sin against us. We are to do this in private with the purpose of winning back the offending Christian so that our fellowship might be preserved. Clearly, this confrontation is to be loving and gentle. (b) Jesus also urges us to examine ourselves and to repent sincerely of our own faults before we confront another about his or her faults. Looking to ourselves first will enable us to confront another in a spirit of understanding and humility. (c) Suppose you or I are on the other end of the confrontation? When we are confronted and admonished because of our own sins, we are to listen and heed the admonition that we may be helped and improved by it.

17. (a) God intends that His Law bring us to godly sorrow and to repentance. Then, in turn, He intends that we receive the assurance of the Gospel that He has forgiven us for Christ's sake and that salvation is ours by

His grace. (b) The condemnation delivered by the unbelieving world leads—at best—to compliance. It often produces resentment and even despair. Worldly condemnation beats people down rather than building them up.

18. The godly sorrow of the Corinthians led them to "eagerness to clear [themselves], indignation, . . . fear . . ., longing, zeal, [and] punishment [readiness to see justice done]." Accept reasonable paraphrases.

19. Paul brought the sin of the Corinthians to their attention so that they could see for themselves how devoted they were to Paul as an apostle through God whom Himself was dealing with them. This goal far overshadowed the sin itself. This does not mean, of course, that Paul was disinterested in those who were injured by the sin or in the spiritual danger in which the wrongdoer had placed himself; of course, Paul shared the Lord's own concern about those who were directly involved. But uppermost in Paul's mind is the spiritual well-being of the entire congregation at Corinth and their response to the Gospel he proclaimed.

20. Of greatest importance to our Lord is a repentant heart that submits to Him and gladly clings to the Gospel of forgiveness.

Day 5 • 2 Corinthians 7:13–16

21. Let participants comment.

22. The Corinthians refreshed the spirit of Titus by their obedience to the Word and to Paul's authority as an apostle of the Lord. The Corinthians received Titus with respect and reverence. This reception encouraged Titus.

23. Boasting selfishly about our own achievements, cleverness, or power is wrong and unworthy of a Christian. However, godly boasting includes boasting about the power of God's Word, God's answer to prayer, the presence of the Lord in our lives, and other such references to the Lord's love and grace. When we can boast in the Lord or of what the Lord has accomplished, it brings glory to Him.

24. Paul could base his complete confidence in the Corinthians following their response to the visitation of Titus. He now knew for certain that the Lord was at work in them, leading them to obey His will as expressed through Paul. Encourage participants to describe experiences when the confidence they placed in other Christians was confirmed and strengthened.

The Collection for the Saints in Jerusalem

2 Corinthians 8:1–9:15

Preparing for the Session

Central Focus

Christian giving, as a response of faith to God's grace in Christ, becomes a means by which God's grace flows even more abundantly through the life of the giver to others.

Objectives

That participants, led by the Holy Spirit, will

1. better understand the evangelical motive and character of Christian giving;
2. desire to grow in the grace of Christian giving; and
3. experience the privilege of Christian giving as a gift of God to the giver.

For the Small-Group Leader

Small-Group Discussion Helps

Day 1 • 2 Corinthians 8:1–7

1. From 1 Corinthians 16:1–4, we learn that the Corinthians were urged to lay aside something for the collection on the first day of each week (implying that Sunday was the regular day on which they gathered for worship). Each believer was to give a portion of the income they had received that week. The money for the collection was to be accumulated in this way so no special fund drive would have to be made when Paul arrived. Couriers chosen by the Corinthians and other congregations would take the money to Jerusalem, carrying letters of introduction from Paul or accompanying him on the journey.

2. The grace of God enabled the Macedonians not only to receive from God but also to respond to Him in rich generosity toward their fellow Christians who were in need—and this despite their own deep poverty! Grace opens up the Christian heart to other people, especially to those in any need. Grace enables us to become gracious.

3. Notice the generosity of the Macedonians! They gave not just as they were able, but beyond what they were able to give. And they did this, not because they themselves were asked to do so (let alone urged to do so), but because they urgently pleaded for the privilege of sharing in this service to those in need.

4. (a) Even before giving (and beyond expectation!), even before begging to be allowed to give their money, the Macedonians first gave themselves to the Lord and to the Lord's servants who were doing the Lord's work. They gave themselves in response to God's grace and love. (b) It's extremely important that we give our own offerings in this same way. To be God-pleasing, our offerings must flow as a response to God's gracious giving to us. Anything less becomes an attempt at a payoff, an obligation, dues, or a favor someone does for God or for others (perhaps with the expectation that the favor will be repaid, possibly with interest).

5. (a) Titus' new job was to complete the collection that had been begun earlier. (b) In verse 7, Paul lists the excellent gifts of grace that were evident among the Corinthians. They include faith (trusting the promises of God, perhaps to an extraordinary degree), speech (confessing and sharing the Word of God), knowledge (understanding of the Christian faith, especially as it focuses on the mighty acts of God seen in Jesus Christ), complete earnestness (a sincerity that demonstrates a connection between words and deeds), and love for Paul (especially over those who were Paul's detractors and accusers).

Day 2 • 2 Corinthians 8:8–15

6. Paul used the example of the Macedonians in order to encourage and even gladden the hearts of the Corinthians. The very attitudes of the Macedonians were what Paul wanted to see in the Corinthians. The Macedonians exhibited an enthusiastic response to the grace of God—the same grace of God that the Corinthians had experienced and continued to enjoy. As you talk about this question with your group, be sure everyone understands that Paul's motive was *not* to shame the Corinthians and thus to manipulate them into responding grudgingly, out of guilt. The rest of this section attests to that.

7. (a) 2 Corinthians 8:9 contrasts what Jesus had as the Son of God (everything!) and what He had as a human being in this world (nothing!). Jesus refers to His poverty in Luke 9:58. (b) John 1:3 declares that the Word, Jesus Christ, is the Creator of all things; Matthew 8:20 quotes Jesus as saying that He has not so much as even a place to lay His head! (c) Philippians 2:6 and 7–8 contrast what Jesus is and what He chose to become for our salvation's sake.

8. Paul chose to remind his readers of the riches and poverty of the Son of God in order to put earthly wealth, and certainly our offerings, into the right perspective, the right context—the tremendous grace of God.

9. Far more important than the amount of our offerings is our motivation for giving those offerings. Paul mentions willingness twice. Such willingness comes from a heart that has been touched by the grace of God. The Lord reads the heart attitude, not the amount written on the face of our check.

10. In 1 Corinthians 16:2, Paul indicates that our giving is to be in accordance with the way God has blessed us; the same point is made in 2 Corinthians 8:12. Our giving ought not to be given *to* a budget or project primarily, but *from* the blessings God has bestowed and *from* a thankful heart. Paul urged that giving not only be proportionate, but regular. Apparently believers in the Early Church were encouraged to bring their offerings when they came to worship, just like we are today.

Day 3 • 2 Corinthians 8:16–24

11. Paul assigned three highly respected people to handle the offering so that no one could accuse him or his coworkers of financial improprieties. His concern isn't hard to understand when we keep in mind that Paul wrote much of this letter to answer the charges of his enemies and detractors.

12. (a) Paul states that he administered the offering to honor the Lord Himself and to show eagerness to help. Paul's motivation was cross-shaped: On the vertical plane, Paul wanted to honor and praise God; on the horizontal plane, he wanted to help those in need in Jerusalem. (b) The best and most God-pleasing reasons haven't changed. Our monetary offerings are part of the total thankoffering of our lives (Romans 12:1) and a means for extending God's kingdom from where we live throughout the world.

13. (a) Paul describes Titus (vv. 17, 23) as enthusiastic and a self-starter. As Paul's partner and fellow worker and as a representative of the churches, Titus is "the glory of Christ." Concerning the unnamed brother mentioned in verses 18–19, Paul comments that his faithful service on behalf of the Gospel is widely known. The churches themselves chose this brother to accompany Paul in bringing the offering to Jerusalem. An unnamed third man is characterized (v. 22) by his zeal and by his confidence in the Christians of Corinth. (b) Paul does not hesitate to praise and commend those who serve the Lord. This does not detract at all from the glory that is given to God. We also can praise and commend those who serve the Lord well, praising and thanking the Lord for their service as we do so. Let participants share their reactions to giving and receiving such praise themselves.

Day 4 • 2 Corinthians 9:1–7

14. Our old nature can dredge up many reasons for not giving thankofferings to the Lord. As examples are given, it might be good to probe deeper to determine what is truly being said when people hesitate to give gladly and sacrificially. Most of the time our old nature appeals to our pride, selfishness, materialism, and even our doubt concerning the promises of God to take care of us.

15. The enthusiasm of the Corinthians set an example for others, especially for the Christians of Macedonia, and stirred others to action. The same can happen today when Christians speak matter-of-factly about the joy they receive from their giving and the blessings they receive from their giving. When we comment in these ways sincerely and without calling attention to ourselves as the givers but to God as the Giver, we are witnessing, not bragging or showing spiritual pride.

16. Paul was fearful that they hadn't followed through on their enthusiastic commitments made one year earlier and thus would embarrass both him and themselves. Paul's greatest fear, however, was that, under the pressure of having to respond when they weren't ready, they would give grudgingly and not gladly.

17. Three characteristics of a God-pleasing offering Paul describes are giving what has been determined thoughtfully and prayerfully, giving without reluctance or second thoughts or resentment, and giving willingly and without a sense of being compelled.

18. **Challenge Question.** Our giving, when motivated by faith and thankfulness, is like planting seed: The more we give, the more we receive from the Lord. This does not necessarily mean that the Lord will bless us

financially; perhaps the blessing will be of another kind altogether. In 2 Corinthians 9:10, Paul refers to how God makes it possible for us to give by supplying us with material blessings so that spiritual blessings may result. Galatians 6:7–9 refers to the principle of sowing and reaping both in negative and in positive terms. The harvest in this passage is spiritual. Philippians 4:19 refers to the fact that God provides materially for His servants as they give generously for His work.

Day 5 • 2 Corinthians 9:8–15

19. 2 Corinthians 8:9 refers to the riches that we receive through Christ, who became poor for our sakes. These riches are not material riches. Indeed, someone can be extremely poor in material things and yet abundantly rich in spiritual things.

20. This question provides an opportunity for even the quietest member of the group to reflect on ways that the Lord has graced his or her life. Provide plenty of opportunity for this. It may be more difficult to describe abounding in good works without sounding boastful. As leader, you may want to acknowledge that while at the same time allowing opportunity for group members to describe ways that the Lord has worked through each of them to bless others. Perhaps if those in your group know one another well, they might comment on specific ways those present have been a blessing to them.

21. Paul assures us that the Lord will provide us with what we need so we can join in the joy of giving and can enjoy the grace of giving. No Christian need say that he or she has nothing to give. Giving to others need not be giving money; it may instead be giving time, or help, or assistance in a way that does not involve money; or caring for someone in a loving way; or giving in any number of other ways. God will give us something we may share and so receive the grace of giving.

22. Our offerings represent one aspect of our response to the Gospel. The offering envelope is part of our confession of faith; by it we are saying that God comes first, as we bring our offerings in response to His grace and mercy and with trust that our God will provide for all of our needs. If we believe that God is worthy of our trust, honor, praise, and thanksgiving, our offerings literally put our money where our mouth is! The opposite is also true. If we give grudgingly, thoughtlessly, and without the cheerfulness of a generous heart, our offerings reflect our attitude toward the Lord—and reveal not a financial problem but a spiritual problem!

23. Paul anticipated that two things would result when the generous contributions of the Corinthians and others had been delivered: (a) People would praise God for the obedience that matched their confession of the Gospel; and (b) People would pray for the givers, who generously shared with those in need.

24. The question, of course, need not be discussed during the session. However, you may invite participants to share any thoughts they have about changed viewpoints concerning giving.

Paul's Defense of His Ministry

2 Corinthians 10:1–18

Preparing for the Session

Central Focus

Paul defends his ministry against those who would judge him by worldly standards and commends his work to the Lord's approval.

Objectives

That participants, led by the Holy Spirit, will

1. know and affirm that the Christian ministry is not to be judged by worldly standards;
2. measure themselves by the standards of God's Word; and
3. boast in the Lord—that is, credit and praise God for what He is able to accomplish through us and others.

For the Small-Group Leader

Small-Group Discussion Helps

Day 1 • 2 Corinthians 10:1

1. (a) Paul's opponents apparently had accused him of being a coward—writing strong words when absent, but acting and speaking in weakness in person. They misrepresented the gentleness, meekness, and tenderness of his Christian character as being weakness and a lack of courage instead. (b) Paul had been patient with the Corinthians and had chosen to admonish them by letter since a stern admonition delivered in person might have permanently damaged his relationship with them, a relationship he treasured. His opponents distorted his patience and consideration, suggesting it was really fear and cowardice.

2. As meekness and gentleness are found in the New Testament, and especially as they are exemplified in Christ, the words carry a connotation of great power held in check by a gentle spirit. (a) In Matthew 11:28–30, Jesus describes Himself as "gentle and lowly in heart"—yet He also calls people to Himself so He might take their burdens and give them rest—hardly the act of a weakling! (b) Matthew 21:1–5 records Jesus' actions on Palm Sunday. Matthew describes Him as gentle, humbly riding on a donkey. A donkey is a gentle animal, unsuitable for warfare. Warriors rode on horseback, not on donkeys. Our Lord's ride took Him to the cross, hardly the destination of a coward.

3. Paul's detractors knew that Paul was far more interested in the Gospel and in the welfare of the Corinthians than in defending himself. As a result, they attacked him in his absence and impugned his authority and his motives. They underestimated the power of meekness and gentleness when possessed by a called servant of God.

4. (a) We are called to display the meekness and gentleness of Christ in our own lives. Doing so exhibits our faith that our Lord will care for us and defend us. Christian meekness and gentleness is not a sign of personal weakness but of a strong faith in God. (b) How do meekness and gentleness serve the cause of the Gospel? This is always a challenge for the Christian. There are times when the Christian's response to others must be to turn the other cheek, while there are other times when that response may encourage people to sin against God—and against us. To say or do nothing in that instance would be wrong. Led by the Spirit, we prayerfully separate our own wishes and feelings from the needs of the other person as we act and speak for the sake of the Gospel. Knowing our own sinfulness and weakness, we rely on our Lord's promise to forgive us when we fail to act in Christlike love. Encourage participants to cite examples of times we're called upon to show Christlike meekness and gentleness.

5. Paul had not been timid; he had been patient, caring, loving, gracious. When he came to Corinth he would be strong, assertive, courageous, and just. Participants may think of other appropriate terms to describe Paul's attitudes.

Day 2 • 2 Corinthians 10:2–4

6. Some in your group may be tempted to use this question as an occasion to accuse others of being fleshly. They may try to air a long list of complaints. You will, of

course, want to discourage that. On the other hand, perhaps not everyone in the group may have experienced what appear to be fleshly approaches to endeavors in Christ's kingdom. You may need to prime the pump by giving some examples yourself. For instance, some Christians consider the pastoral office as merely another job to be filled by using application forms and search committees. This can turn the God-given office of the holy ministry into merely another occupation. Or consider the issue of Christian stewardship. Sometimes those in charge are tempted to use fear, guilt, and shame to motivate giving—anything to increase the budget. The same questionable practices can be used to get people to serve on committees, teach Sunday School, or sing in the choir. These fleshly approaches run counter to the Gospel and fail to honor Christ.

7. The contrast between Christian standards and beliefs and the world's standards and beliefs are becoming increasingly apparent. Let participants name some. They range from sexual morality to the view taken of marriage to beliefs about business ethics to the value put on human life (including the lives of the unborn and the elderly).

8. Paul's "distance personality" and "close-up personality" were one and the same. (a) In Acts 15:1–2, Paul and Barnabas sharply opposed the opinion of the circumcision party, those who insisted that circumcision was necessary for salvation. (b) In Galatians 2:11–16, Paul describes his confrontation of the apostle Peter. Peter had acted hypocritically and in doing so had denied the Gospel—eating with "unclean" Gentile Christians until some Jews arrived, and then refusing their company. Paul clearly treasured the truth and spoke up for it when the circumstances required. However, he did this with great love and sensitivity toward his hearers and for the sake of the Gospel.

9. **Challenge Question.** Paul's opponents were using the worldly weapons of unfounded accusations, character attacks, gossip, and self-promotion.

10. (a) Paul used the weapons of the Christian warrior described in Ephesians 6:13–18. These include truth, righteousness, the peace of Christ, faith, the assurance of salvation, the Word of God, and prayer. (b) These spiritual weapons are the right ones since we are in a fight not with human opponents but with spiritual opponents led by the devil himself. To engage spiritual opponents we need spiritual weapons! (c) These weapons are capable of destroying false arguments and pretensions.

Day 3 • 2 Corinthians 10:5–6

11. (a) In the wilderness, Christ did not use the great power that was His as the Son of God. Instead, He submitted Himself to the will of the Father, even when confronting evil. The weapon that Christ used in the wilderness temptations was the Word of God. In each of the three final temptations, Jesus quoted God's Word. Paul did the same thing, pushing aside every human resource to submit to the Lord's power. (b) The Word of God has a power of penetration that far exceeds any human weapon. God's Word penetrates to the heart, to the inner thoughts and motives of a person. Since it is God's Word, it works effectively against spiritual as well as human opponents.

12. **Challenge Question.** Paul expects the Corinthian believers to get their own house in order. He anticipated that he would have to take strong action against disobedience and rebellion. But the believers who accepted his authority and submitted to it had sins that he urged them to address before he arrived. Sin matters—even in the lives of committed Christians. It hurts us, it damages our witness, it can wreck relationships, and it can even drive a wedge between us and our Savior. Paul wanted the Corinthians to realize this and escape sin's dangers through repentance and faith.

13. When the Law condemns us, we take God's Word seriously. Our Lord wants us to receive that Word, recognize our sin and admit our guilt, turn to Him for the forgiveness He promises to grant us in Christ, and by His power amend what is evil in our hearts and lives.

Day 4 • 2 Corinthians 10:7–11

14. The Lord had called Paul as His apostle, with particular responsibility for bringing the Gospel to the Gentiles. To carry out that assignment, God gave Paul a corresponding authority. That authority, however, was not to be used arbitrarily but to accomplish the purpose of Paul's ministry—to build up the Church among the Gentiles. Though Paul at times had to use the tearing-down function of the Law, he always was working toward his primary goal—edifying (building up) the Church.

15. Like Paul, we also are to build up the Church. We do that in many different ways. (a) We edify the church when we work patiently with one another, helping one another grow beyond weaknesses by patient teaching and encouragement. (b) We edify the Church when we

build ourselves up by seeking an ever-closer relationship with Christ. (c) We edify the Church when we desire and use the gifts that the Spirit distributes among Christians for the common good. (If no one in the group mentions it, point out that the Scripture tells of other practices by which we can edify one another. In one way or another, all involve bringing the Word of God to bear on individual human hearts.)

16. Clearly, Paul's opponents were preoccupied with personal power. They were impressed only with external demonstrations of such power and seem to have concerned themselves not at all with truth and righteousness. In this they revealed that they belong to the world system kept in place by sin and Satan. They follow this world's agenda and are not of God.

17. Paul, on the other hand, was unconcerned about building his personal power or prestige among the Corinthians. He cared about proclaiming Christ as Lord and Savior among the Corinthians. Period. Paul submerged his own personality, while he held up Christ, and Him crucified, to the Corinthians.

Day 5 • 2 Corinthians 10:12–18

18. (a) When people compare themselves with themselves, they can't lose by the comparison. They make themselves the measure of all things. Two verses from the Old Testament may be helpful here. Proverbs 3:7 says, "Be not wise in your own eyes; fear the LORD and turn away from evil"; Isaiah 5:21 warns, "Woe to those who are wise in their own eyes and shrewd in their own sight!" (b) Making ourselves the measure of all things is unwise because doing it distorts our view of reality. On the other hand, comparing ourselves to others is not wise, either—and for the same reason. We will always find someone who from a worldly viewpoint seems more sinful than we consider ourselves to be, and we will always be able to find someone who lives a more holy life—at least outwardly. Only one standard will give us a true picture both of ourselves and of our motives. This is the standard God sets for us in His Word.

19. Paul confined himself to the field that God Himself had given him, and he served there with his whole heart. We, too, would do well to concentrate on those tasks God has assigned to us. This applies to congregations, entities within congregations, and individuals. God has given us enough to do in our own field without encroaching on the fields he has given to others. Let participants suggest specific examples.

20. Paul hoped that the Corinthians could get past the present crisis, grow in their faith, and then reach out beyond themselves so that the Gospel could spread to regions and nations beyond them. Notice, however, that Paul intended to focus the Gospel proclamation in areas where people had not yet heard it (v. 16).

21. When people boast about themselves and their own achievements or position, their boasting is foolish and out of place. But we may boast when our boasting gives credit where it is due—to God Himself. Boasting pleases God when it results in His glory, praise, and thanksgiving to Him. When we boast in the Lord, we are making the joyful acknowledgement that nothing happens by accident, but that God guides, directs, and blesses our lives in Christ. And that's something to boast about!

Paul's Foolish Boasting

2 Corinthians 11:1–12:21

Preparing for the Session

Central Focus

Though reluctant, Paul feels driven to boast, to speak about himself, his accomplishments, and his weaknesses so he might defend the ministry the Lord had given him against the false charges of his opponents in Corinth.

Objectives

That participants, led by the Holy Spirit, will

1. understand more about Paul's personal career as an apostle through the information he provides as he "boasts";
2. be encouraged by the lesson God taught Paul through his thorn in the flesh—that God's grace is sufficient for us as we go about the tasks He gives to us; and
3. give glory and honor to God for what He accomplishes through us.

For the Small-Group Leader

Small-Group Discussion Helps

Day 1 • 2 Corinthians 11:1–12

1. As Paul wrote the section you studied this week, his emotions are exposed and raw. He cares deeply about the Corinthians. In verse 2, he compares the Corinthians' relationship with Christ to that of the intimate relationship between a loving husband (Christ) and his bride (a "pure virgin"—the Corinthians). Paul is the spiritual father who has promised the bride to her husband. (In a day of arranged marriages, such a picture would have seemed natural.) Paul watches over his spiritual daughter, betrothed to the Lord. However, she has been led astray and is in danger of betraying her love for the Lord.

2. Paul compares the deceitfulness of the false teachers toward the Corinthians with Satan's temptation of Eve. Obviously, in referencing the fall, Paul is warning the Corinthians about the seriousness of the lies and false accusations of the false teachers. These teachers have become instruments of the devil!

3. (a) The Bereans set an example for believers of all time. They did not gullibly accept the claims of anyone who came with a message they said came from God. Instead, they compared the message with what was in the Holy Scriptures. The Bereans discovered that what Paul was telling them lined up with the Old Testament Scriptures. This may not always be the case; our Lord wants us to check the teaching we hear to make sure it is in line with what God has already revealed to us in the Scriptures. (b) If we find that a teacher's doctrines do not match the Scriptures, we need to speedily and firmly show that teacher to the door. The believer is to have no part in false teachings or with those who advocate them.

4. Despite Paul's deep knowledge of the Scriptures and his educated background, he apparently had not been trained in public speaking. We read a similar comment in 1 Corinthians 2:1—"I . . . did not come . . . with lofty speech." Nevertheless, Paul had something the false teachers did not have—knowledge given to him by Christ, a knowledge that exalted not himself but the Lord. Obviously, even in less important matters, substance matters far more important than style. Yet, too often, false teachers seek to substitute style for substance, and people are deceived. The truth of the Gospel is far more important than the one who brings the message or the way he presents the message. Indeed, as every pastor knows, it is too easy for the messenger to get in the way of the message!

5. Paul "lowered" himself in the eyes of the Corinthians by coming too cheap! He did not ask for any financial support from the Corinthians because he did not want to become a burden to them.

6. Paul's approach—teaching without pay—would indicate that, unlike the false teachers, he was not interested in their money but in them. The false teachers apparently charged the Corinthians for their services, and yet claimed to be equal to Paul (v. 12).

Day 2 • 2 Corinthians 11:13–21a

7. (a) False teachers today, as in Paul's day, often appear attractive, and their message can be appealing. They may seem very holy and righteous. Even strong Christians may be taken in at first by their outward appearance. Participants may think of the leaders of various religious cults and non-Christian religions who make a positive initial impression. (b) There is only one way to protect oneself against the deceptions of false teachers, to have the ability to "distinguish good from evil," and that is to grow in God's Word. We need to immerse ourselves in the truth of that Word, not just skim lightly over the surface by attending church occasionally. We must become mature Christians, knowledgeable of God's truth, if we are to recognize falsehood despite its initial outward appearance of truth.

8. In contrast with the false teachers, Paul had treated the Corinthians with respect. He had not abused them or pushed them around. He had not taken advantage of them when they were weak and immature. He had patiently built them up as they grew toward Christian maturity. (a) The false teachers sought to enslave the Corinthians, exploit them, take advantage of them, push themselves forward, and even to slap them in the face. (b) Apparently the Corinthians were only too ready to be impressed by the self-assurance and big talk of these false teachers. Perhaps the Corinthians lacked confidence in God or had allowed their spiritual strength to be drained off by Satan's temptations and lies. (c) Paul admits that he and his companions were too weak for the kinds of tactics practiced by the false teachers—an accusation made by the false teachers and hurled back at them now by Paul. Paul's tender pastoral approach was not, of course, weakness. It was the respect and love that a servant of God shows toward those whom the Lord calls him to serve.

Day 3 • 2 Corinthians 11:21b–33

9. Paul answers the false teachers by bringing up their boasts and then showing how his life matches and far surpasses anything about which they feel they can boast. They say, "We are Hebrews, Israelites, offspring of Abraham, and servants of Christ." Paul responds, "I am a Hebrew also, an Israelite also, an offspring of Abraham, and much more a servant of Christ than they!" Paul then adds specific details about his service for Christ.

10. (a) That Paul was "better" than his opponents was proven by the fact that he worked harder, was imprisoned more frequently, and was flogged more severely. He was exposed to death frequently, and was beaten, stoned, and shipwrecked. Paul faced dangers from rivers, bandits, his own countrymen, Gentiles, dangers in the city and country, dangers at sea, and dangers from false brothers. The physical deprivations that Paul endured included going without sleep. He also had known hunger and thirst, cold and nakedness. (b) All of these experiences show the complete and total devotion and dedication of Paul to his Lord and to the ministry to which the Lord had called him. Paul's willingness to face dangers testifies to his total trust and confidence in God to protect and deliver him. The deprivations Paul experienced show that he would allow nothing to prevent him from carrying out the work to which God had called him.

11. (a) Besides all of the physical trials Paul faced, he also had the daily pastoral concern for all the churches that were under his care. (b) Paul cared deeply about the needs of the churches. When the believers were weak, so was he. When they were led into sin (as the Corinthians had been), he burned inwardly in his grief and concern. All of this shows that Paul was a deeply devoted and caring pastor.

12. (a) Surprisingly, Paul makes his greatest boast in his weakness. Normally, we feel most ashamed of our greatest weaknesses and make every effort to keep others from seeing them. But Paul boasted about his weakness—that is, he openly acknowledged it and pointed it out—because God's grace at work in him was all the more evident because of his weaknesses. God's power working through him appeared all the more clearly because of his weaknesses. Paul's weakness made it clear to him and to others that all credit for what he accomplished belonged to God and not to him. (b) The example of weakness to which Paul refers came early in his ministry (Acts 9:19–25) when he preached in the synagogue in Damascus. The Jews were so infuriated that they watched for him day and night in order to find an opportunity to kill him. Paul had to slip past them by being lowered in a basket from a window in the city wall—hardly a dignified exit! Yet Paul did not mind sharing this humiliating incident because it had happened for the sake of the Gospel, and it proved his point about his weakness. Paul could boast about such circumstances because the Lord and His Gospel were glorified even while Paul was not. (c) Letting people see us as we actually are rather than as the way we would like

to be takes courage. But such transparent honesty will do the same in our case as it did in the case of Paul—it will shift attention from us to God and His power, which is where the emphasis belongs. Such honesty also will cause people to think more of us, not less.

Day 4 • 2 Corinthians 12:1–10

13. Paul does not identify the "man in Christ" whose vision he now relates. He seems to make a distinction between this man and himself in verse 5. On the other hand, verse 7 seems to suggest that the vision he relates is his own, after all. His familiarity with the facts given in verses 2b–4 also suggest that he is relating his own experience. Because of his detailed knowledge about this experience, and because Paul did not mind using himself as an example of the Lord's power, the person Paul is describing is quite probably Paul himself.

14. Paul is not certain whether the experience he is describing was a bodily experience or whether it was a vision in which the spirit left the body. But he is certain that *God* gave the experience and revealed *His* glory through it. It was an experience that glorified God rather than the person who experienced it. When Christians boast, Paul says elsewhere, we are to boast in the Lord.

15. Paul's boasting was guided by these principles: His boasting exposed his own weaknesses so that God's grace and power might be exposed by comparison. What he boasted about was the truth, not an embellishment or distortion of the truth. His boasting would not cause anyone to think more of him than was warranted by the facts.

16. (a) So that Paul would not think more highly of himself than he ought to have thought because of the special revelations and privileges given to him (plus his many pastoral gifts), Paul experienced a "thorn in the flesh." (b) We cannot know much about this "thorn" from the brief reference Paul makes here and does not repeat elsewhere. However, we can know that it was physical ("in the flesh"), that it was sent by Satan (although God permitted Satan to afflict Paul in this way), that it was continuing, and that it tormented him. Paul never describes it beyond this. The "thorn" was severe enough that it was a constant reminder to Paul of where the power and glory lay—not with him, but with the Lord. Paul could not brag about his own power or abilities. The "thorn" prevented that. Instead, he knew that any power he had came from Christ. (c) Paul's trials and difficulties, especially his "thorn," spoke loudly of God's grace in Paul's life. Paul, weak as he was, could display Christ's power at work in him. Some in your discussion group may have experienced many trials and difficulties. Even those who have experienced few trials nevertheless share in the difficulties of living in a fallen world where trials can come at any time. Some in your group may be in the throes of a trial right now. Some may be hurting and some may even struggle with the temptation to bitterness. Certainly some will have experienced the grace of God even in the midst of difficult times. Be sensitive to the fact that this is not a therapy group, while, at the same time, allowing group members to show Christian care and concern for one another. (d) Paul says he came to "delight" in his weaknesses, realizing that God's power could come through most strongly when his own strength did not get in the way.

Day 5 • 2 Corinthians 12:11–21

17. The miraculous deeds done by Paul and the other apostles marked them as authentic apostles of Christ. The power with which Christ Himself had done miraculous signs rested also upon His messengers.

18. When Paul came to the Corinthians, he purposely did not depend on them for his support. He did not intend to be a burden to them. Instead of regarding this as a positive sign of his unselfish servant attitude, at least some of the Corinthians apparently held it against him. So, with a good deal of sarcasm, Paul asks them to forgive him for the "wrong" of not making himself a burden to them by charging them for his ministry—like the false teachers were doing. Paul gives three reasons for choosing not to be a burden to the Corinthians: to demonstrate that he wasn't coveting their possessions, but rather wanted their hearts; because, like a parent, he did not think it right to be supported by his spiritual children; and because of his unselfish love for them.

19. Paul and Titus were not motivated by a desire to exploit their ministry among the Corinthians to gain power, money, or possessions. Their ministry was not for their own benefit but so that the Corinthians might benefit from the Gospel.

20. Paul intends to strengthen the Corinthians in their knowledge and faith. He wants them to earnestly repent of their former sins and leave such sins behind them so they can grow in the Gospel and go forward with the Gospel.

21. Encourage participants to share their answers with the group.

Paul's Impending Visit to Corinth

2 Corinthians 13:1–14

Preparing for the Session

Central Focus

Paul is now ready to make his long-delayed visit to Corinth. As he prepares for this visit, he speaks a final warning as well as assurance and love for the repentant.

Objectives

That participants, led by the Holy Spirit, will

1. rejoice that God's ultimate intention is to forgive and restore us when we sin so we might receive His grace and be saved;
2. regard the Gospel and those who proclaim it as having the power of God; and
3. examine themselves daily so that they remain in the faith and exhibit that faith in love toward others.

For the Small-Group Leader

Small-Group Discussion Helps

Day 1 • 2 Corinthians 13:1–4

1. Paul promises that when he visits the believers in Corinth he will not spare those guilty of "quarreling, jealousy, anger, hostility, slander, gossip, conceit, and disorder" (12:20), nor those who have followed the deceivers.

2. In Luke 10:6, Jesus clearly says that those who speak His Word in His name speak His very words. In and of himself, Paul had no power. But by virtue of Christ's call to apostleship, Paul carried the authority and power of Christ Himself.

3. Christ did indeed appear to be weak to those who put Him to death. He had intentionally taken the form of a servant and made Himself of no account to earn salvation for us. The greatest "evidence" of Christ's weakness, Paul asserts, is His crucifixion, a most humiliating and public kind of death. Yet, the cross and open tomb ultimately display God's power at its zenith—by death Christ defeated death, hell, sin, and Satan.

4. (a) How comforting to know that God's power is not limited by our weakness but that His power actually works through us in our weakness to accomplish His saving purposes. Encourage participants to share their responses to this question. (b) **Challenge Question.** Paul declares that his own weakness does not limit God's dynamic, dynamite power to work through him. That reminder should also have been good news to the Corinthians. The Corinthians had plenty of evidence that they, certainly, were weak. The sins and shortcomings Paul cites in 12:20–21 revealed their weakness. But God's power is not limited by our weakness. Help group members to personalize this truth.

Day 2 • 2 Corinthians 13:5–6

5. (a) The sacred Scriptures are the only source and norm for faith and life. (b) Nevertheless, saving faith involves more than knowing in our heads the facts about God and His plan for our salvation. This knowledge must enter our hearts and be translated into attitudes and behavior, especially behavior toward others. Such a faith, one that generates attitudes and behavior consistent with God's will, reveals itself as a genuine faith. Faith, and not the results it produces, is what saves us since faith clings only and always to God's grace. But genuine faith will always produce God-pleasing attitudes and behaviors.

6. (a) Paul commanded Titus to use the sharpness of the Law on the people of Crete so that they would see their sins and repent. In this way, their faith would become sound and solid. This is always God's intention when He speaks the Law to our hearts. Of course, human beings can harden their hearts and rebel. Many do. But that is not God's will or His purpose in giving us the Law and personalizing it in our lives. (b) Let volunteers share their thoughts. Our flesh often rebels at being shown our sin. However, when we realize that God in genuine kindness and concern for our eternal welfare wants to lead us to repentance (Romans 2:4), we can respond as He would have us respond.

7. Regular self-examination and confession of sins can help us avoid falling into vice (sins of habit) and into open and impenitent sin that puts us in spiritual danger and damages or destroys our Christian witness. Refer the group to 1 Corinthians 11:31 as time will allow.

8. If the Corinthians are in Christ, then they will recog-

nize that Paul also is in Christ and that his apostleship is genuine. Paul was the one, after all, who had brought the Corinthians to saving faith.

Day 3 • 2 Corinthians 13:7–8

9. Paul prays these words for the sake of the Corinthian believers. He does not pray them for his own sake or his own honor.

10. (a) God's truth is centered in Jesus; the Gospel is the truth—God's Word about Jesus. (b) The first part of Galatians 2:14 identifies the truth with the Gospel—the Good News of forgiveness of sins and eternal life in Christ Jesus. (c) 2 Thessalonians 2:10 says that the truth saves us; again, a clear reference to the suffering, death, and resurrection of Jesus Christ for our sins.

11. The powerful weapon that Paul has to counter his own weaknesses, the trials he had to endure, and the lies of the false teachers is *the truth*. Encourage participants to respond to the question and to personalize their response.

Day 4 • 2 Corinthians 13:9–10

12. (a) Paul's enemies prefer that they be strong and the Corinthians be weak. Paul, however, would prefer that the Corinthians be strong and he weak. (b) Ephesians 3:17–19 describes the completeness of the Christian as that of growing in every direction in grasping the love of Christ to the point of being filled with this knowledge up to "the fullness of God." (c) This completeness in Christian love and knowledge is accomplished through the work of the Holy Spirit in the heart. Knowing this, Paul prays that the Holy Spirit will complete His work in the Christians of Ephesus.

13. Paul wrote the "hard things" in a letter so that, given time and opportunity to respond, the Corinthians might repent and believe. Then, when Paul came in person, he would not have to be harsh in rebuking sin, but might use his authority to build up the faith of the Corinthians in a gentle, loving way.

14. (a) The purpose of Paul's ministerial authority or of any pastor's authority is to bring people, by the power of the Holy Spirit, to a saving relationship with Jesus Christ and to build them up in their faith in Christ. (b) Christ gives His ministers today the same tools Paul used—Word and Sacrament, specifically Law and Gospel. The goal of every sermon, even if the pastor must first deal with the sins of the people, is to show them the good news of God's mercy, freely given, and God's love, fully revealed, in the life, death, and resurrection of Jesus Christ.

Day 5 • 2 Corinthians 13:11–14

15. Let volunteers share their thoughts. If no one mentions it, point out the great optimism with which Paul concludes. He is confident that God can accomplish much in the Corinthians.

16. (a) The words that suggest Paul's hopefulness concerning the outcome are "and the God of love and peace will be with you." This is not a wish, but a confidence he has in the promises of God as he closes this letter. (b) Let volunteers comment. The same God of love and peace who indwelt the Corinthians is also with us. As the empowered people of God, we always live under the love and peace of God, and that gives us great hope for every circumstance of life.

17. **Challenge Question.** The answers are not, of course, given in verse 11. Yet they are present throughout the letter. Suggested responses include, but are not limited to the following: (a) Aim for restoration by taking to heart what Paul has written, by hearing the Law of God, by recognizing sin for the terrible thing it is, and, by the power of the Spirit, repenting and believing in the promises of God. (b) Comfort one another because our comfort comes from the Lord Himself and can only build you up, not tear you down. (c) Agree with one another by heeding the words of this letter, sharing in repentance, and celebrating together the love and mercy of your forgiving God and Savior. (d) Live in peace because the God of peace rules your hearts and lives, and you can show it!

18. We express our Christian love and affection for one another with words. But, for such words to be believable, we reinforce them with attitudes and actions. People look to our attitudes and actions to affirm or to nullify what we say with our words.

19. Let volunteers share their thoughts. The apostolic blessing highlights some of the most precious attributes that God reveals to us about Himself. Throughout this letter, the message of God's free gift of forgiveness and salvation predominates, even when Paul rebukes the Corinthians. After all, only a loving parent cares enough to discipline his or her wayward children. The fellowship in Corinth had been broken by sin. Nevertheless, the Holy Spirit was still at work, creating fellowship. Grace, love, and fellowship are not mere theological abstractions. They describe the way God thinks about us and works within us. His grace is greater than anything that might separate us from Him. His fellowship enfolds us in His arms, and those arms link us with one another.

20. Give every participant an opportunity to identify that verse or concept from 2 Corinthians that has had the greatest impact upon him or her, but don't force anyone to share.